MILL ON LIBERTY

MILL ON LIBERTY

C. L. TEN

CLARENDON PRESS · OXFORD
1980

Oxford University Press, Walton Street, Oxford OX2 6DP

OXFORD   LONDON   GLASGOW
NEW YORK   TORONTO   MELBOURNE   WELLINGTON
KUALA LUMPUR   SINGAPORE   HONG KONG   TOKYO
DELHI   BOMBAY   CALCUTTA   MADRAS   KARACHI
NAIROBI   DAR ES SALAAM   CAPE TOWN

Published in the United States
by Oxford University Press, New York

British Library Cataloguing in Publication Data

Ten, C L
    Mill on liberty.
    1. Mill, John Stuart — Politics and government
    2. Liberty
    I. Title
    323.44′092′4   JC223.M66   80.40977

    ISBN 0-19-824643-9
    ISBN 0-19-824644-7 Pbk

*Set in Great Britain by
Express Litho Service (Oxford).*

*Printed in Great Britain by
Richard Clay and Company Limited,
The Chaucer Press, Suffolk*

*To my parents, and
to Kiang and Hsiu-Hui*

Preface

I was first introduced to Mill's essay *On Liberty* when, as an undergraduate at the University of Singapore, I attended Rusi Khan's lucid lectures. These lectures and Frank Cioffi's lively participation in the ensuing discussion gave me an abiding interest in the essay. Since then I have benefited from the commentaries of others even when I have disagreed with them. I would like to acknowledge in particular the works of John Rees, Alan Ryan, and Richard Wollheim. The *Mill News Letter* has been a source of very useful information. The splendid work done by John M. Robson and his associates at the University of Toronto Press in the publication of the *Collected Works of John Stuart Mill* has been an enormous help. Like many others working in the areas of moral, legal, and political philosophy, I am greatly indebted to, and have been influenced by, the writings of H. L. A. Hart. I have also learnt much from conversations and correspondence with him. In many hours of discussion with John Gray, I have been helped towards a better understanding of Mill's arguments. I have also profited from conversations with Alan Montefiore and Joseph Raz. J. W. N. Watkins read an early version of part of Chapter 8, and gave me helpful comments. I read a version of Chapter 4 to a seminar in Oxford conducted by John Gray, Alan Ryan, and W. L. Weinstein and gained much from their comments. I should also like to record my appreciation of the encouragement given to me by David Spitz whose untimely death has robbed us of a dedicated teacher and a champion of the Millian values of liberty and tolerance. Monash University granted me study leave in 1979 without which I would not have been able to complete this book. I am also grateful to Balliol College for extending to me the hospitality of its Senior Common Room while I was in Oxford. My wife and daughter had to put up with me more than usual when I was writing the book.

I wish to thank the respective editors and publishers for permission to use material from the following papers of mine:

'Mill on Self-Regarding Conduct', *Philosophy,* 1968; 'Mill and Liberty', *Journal of the History of Ideas,* 1969; 'Crime and Immorality', *Modern Law Review,* 1969; 'Paternalism and Morality', *Ratio,* 1971; 'Mill's Stable Society', *The Mill News Letter,* 1971; 'Enforcing a Shared Morality', *Ethics,* 1972; 'The Liberal Theory of the Open Society', in Dante Germino and Klaus von Beyme (eds.), *The Open Society in Theory and Practice* (Martinus Nijhofff, The Hague, 1974); Review of Gertrude Himmelfarb, *On Liberty and Liberalism: The Case of John Stuart Mill, Political Theory,* 1975; 'Utilitarianism and Self-Regarding Conduct', *Australasian Journal of Philosophy,* 1977; 'Blasphemy and Obscenity', *British Journal of Law and Society,* 1978.

Melbourne, February 1980.

Contents

x *Contents*

1

Introduction

Whenever liberalism is attacked today, John Stuart Mill's name will almost certainly be mentioned. Often indeed the conservative and radical critics of liberalism have seen in Mill's essay *On Liberty*[1] the embodiment of all the liberal errors and vices they wish to expose. Thus when Wilmoore Kendall speaks of the fallacies of the open society, it is on Mill's alleged fallacies that he dwells.[2] Similarly, when Robert Paul Wolff attacks the poverty of liberalism, he devotes a great deal of his time to laying bare the purported confusions, inconsistencies, and gross inadequacies of Mill's essay.[3] Like Mill's critics, I too regard this essay as the most eloquent expression of the liberal theory of the open society. But unlike them I am generally sympathetic to his values and I have tried to expound his case for liberty as clearly and fully as I can. The foundations Mill provides for his liberal theory have some faults, but a careful study of the essay will reveal that these are often quite different from those which conservative and radical critics of his have been inclined to stress.

Different interpretations of the essay have been given. Many of these are conflicting and yet each is, taken on its own, often quite plausible. It is therefore necessary not just to give a plausible account but also to test it against alternative interpretations. I have built my exposition of Mill on an examination of various views of his work. This approach would have won the approval of Mill himself. In the essay he claims that in complicated subjects like morals, religion, and politics, 'three-fourths of the arguments for every disputed opinion consist in dispelling the appearances which favour some opinion different from it.' (p. 96.) But there is also the danger of cluttering one's text with too many details and of being side-tracked by the arguments of others. I have therefore had to ignore some interesting papers, although wherever possible I have at the appropriate places referred

1

to them in footnotes, and sometimes also added brief comments there.

I

The essay *On Liberty* is concerned with the limits of the coercive power which the state and society may legitimately exercise over the individual. In the past, Mill says, the stuggle for individual liberty was waged against tyrannical governments. This battle was won with the establishment of democracy where the government was responsible to, and removable by, the people. It was then believed that the government could be trusted with power as it was the people who dictated the use to which such power was to be put. But this belief proved to be false. In a democracy the people who had power were the majority, and the liberty of the rest of society was still not secure against 'the tyranny of the majority' and against the power which a government, subservient to current majority view, might exercise. Individual liberty in such a situation was threatened both by oppressive laws and by the use of extra-legal means to impose the prevailing views and practices on everyone. This extra-legal coercion was far more pervasive and insidious than the use of legal penalities because 'it leaves fewer means of escape, penetrating much more deeply into the details of life, and enslaving the soul itself.' (p. 68.)

To defend individual liberty a limit must be set to the extent of legitimate social intervention both by the state and by society. This limit should not depend on the 'likings and dislikings' of the dominant group in society. In this respect most of those who held enlightened views had been at fault even when they were defending the freedom of dissentients. For they did not question the right of society to impose what it liked, and to suppress what it disliked. Instead they merely addressed themselves to the question of what society ought to like or dislike. They were interested in substituting a set of more enlightened views and practices for less enlightened ones, rather than in challenging the principle that one group in society had the right to impose its tastes and standards, however cultivated, on all the rest.

There is no recognized principle defining the proper limits

of social intervention with the freedom of individuals, and Mill put forward his 'one very simple principle' to remedy this.

That principle is, that the sole end for which mankind are warranted, individually or collectively, in interfering with the liberty of action of any of their number, is self-protection. That the only purpose for which power can be rightfully exercised over any member of a civilised community, against his will, is to prevent harm to others. His own good, either physical or moral, is not a sufficient warrant. He cannot rightfully be compelled to do or forbear because it will be better for him to do so, because it will make him happier, because, in the opinions of others, to do so would be wise, or even right. These are good reasons for remonstrating with him, or reasoning with him, or persuading him, or entreating him, but not for compelling him, or visiting him with any evil in case he do otherwise. To justify that, the conduct from which it is desired to deter him must be calculated to produce evil to some one else. The only part of the conduct of any one, for which he is amenable to society, is that which concerns others. In the part which merely concerns himself, his independence is, of right, absolute. Over himself, over his own body and mind, the individual is sovereign. (pp. 72–3.)

Mill explains the scope of his liberty principle. It applies only to 'human beings in the maturity of their faculties' and not to children, or to 'those backward states of society in which the race itself may be considered in its nonage'. In these 'backward states' people are not 'capable of being improved by free and equal discussion'. The test, then, is one of capability rather than willingness. It is also a test that is applied to ascertain the general level of society and not to particular individuals. This is presumably because Mill believes that where people in a society generally have the required capacity, those who lack it can aquire it through their interaction with others in an atmosphere of freedom. It is also evident that the level of the capacity is not pitched very high because Mill asserts that it has been reached long ago by 'all nations with whom we need here concern ourselves'.

Mill's liberty principle specifies that where the individual is 'sovereign', the type of intervention in his conduct that is unacceptable involves the use of punishment and compulsion. He is careful to point out that argument, persuasion and other methods of non-coercive influence are permitted. Indeed later in the essay he pleads for an increase in the exercise of such non-coercive influences, and repeats his condemnation of the use of 'whips and scourges, either of the literal or metaphorical sort' (p. 132). Throughout this book I shall use the terms 'intervention' and 'interference' to mean 'coercive intervention' and coercive interference'.

Mill's principle invokes a distinction between conduct which 'merely concerns' the individual himself and conduct which 'concerns others'. This distinction is commonly restated as that between self-regarding and other-regarding actions. The term 'self-regarding' is used by Mill himself although he does not employ the term 'other-regarding'. His claim is that society is never justified in interfering with self-regarding conduct. But society may be justified in interfering with other-regarding actions which fall within the limits of social intervention. From this it does not follow that intervention in such acts is always justified. For example, the harm caused by intervention may sometimes be greater than the harm to others inflicted by other-regarding actions.

II

How does Mill defend his liberty principle? He states that his case for liberty is not based on 'the idea of abstract right, as a thing independent of utility'. 'I regard utility as the ultimate appeal on all ethical questions; but it must be utility in the largest sense grounded on the permanent interests of man as a progressive being.'[4] The nature of Mill's ultimate value, 'utility in the largest sense', is the subject of much dispute. The main bone of contention is over whether, or to what extent, Mill is a consistent utilitarian.

Utilitarianism is a consequentialist doctrine in that it judges the rightness or wrongness of an act solely in terms of its good or bad consequences when compared with those of alternative acts. The desirable or good consequences of the act consist in the production of utility or happiness. The happiness here is that of all those affected by the act. A right act is thus that which among all the available alternatives maximizes utility or happiness. This standard is often referred to as the principle of utility. Classical utilitarianism, as propounded by Jeremy Bentham and others, conceives of happiness hedonistically as pleasure or the balance of pleasure over pain, and pleasure is regarded as a psychological or mental state. Classical utilitarianism can be distinguished from preference utilitarianism in which the notion of maximizing utility or happiness is reinterpreted as, or replaced by, the notion of maximizing the satisfaction of preferences or desires.[5] Maximizing the satisfaction of desires involves taking into account both the number of desires satisfied and their intensity. When a person gets whatever he wants his desires are satisfied. But it does not follow that he experiences a pleasurable sensation. He may want others to inflict some pain or discomfort on him. The notion of desire is also used in a wide sense such that a person's desire can be satisfied without his knowledge or even after his death. If I desire to be cremated when I die, then my desire is satisfied if I am cremated even though I shall not have any experience when it happens.[6]

Both classical and preference utilitarianism are versions of act utilitarianism in which each act is assessed by the utilitarian standard of maximizing happiness or utility. They are to be distinguished from rule utilitarianism in which the utilitarian standard is not applied directly to particular acts but to rules or institutions. In rule utilitarianism the right act is that which falls under the best rule. A particular right act may not maximize utility, but it belongs to a class of acts, which, if generally performed, will maximize utility. Unless otherwise stated I shall use the term 'utilitarianism' throughout this book to refer to act utilitarianism in both the classical and preference versions.

The question then is whether Mill's defence of liberty is consistently utilitarian. I shall argue that there are significant non-utilitarian elements in his case for liberty, and I shall try to identify some of these. A crude, and somewhat inaccurate, way of describing Mill's position is to say that he was a straightforward utilitarian at the level of other-regarding actions, but that he was not a utilitarian at the level of self-regarding conduct. This is inaccurate for several reasons. First, the distinction between self- and other-regarding conduct is problematic, and I shall argue that Mill's defence of liberty does not depend on there being two different areas of a person's conduct which have very different effects. His case depends on distinguishing between different reasons for interfering with the individual's conduct in any area. Certain reasons are always ruled out as irrelevant, but there is one reason, the prevention of harm to others, which is always relevant.[7] Secondly, even when interference is designed to prevent harm to others, Mill's concern is not simply to minimize the harm (or maximize the prevention of harm). He is also interested in the way the harm is spread out or distributed between different people, and the distributive principle he gestures towards seems to be independent of utilitarianism. A utilitarian is ultimately only interested in maximizing happiness or, where appropriate, minimizing harm and suffering. The way in which the happiness or suffering is distributed is only of secondary importance: it is important only in so far as it affects the total. An unequal distribution is not intrinsically worse than an equal one.

So there is no simple and accurate description of Mill's position. But the crude account will serve as a rough guide which will be qualified and refined as we proceed.

III

In Chapter 2 I discuss Mill's notion of self-regarding conduct. According to the traditional interpretation, self-regarding conduct does not affect others at all except with their consent. But this interpretation is mistaken for Mill readily concedes that self-regarding conduct has certain adverse effects on others. His argument is that a principled defence of individual liberty will lead us to discount these effects on others. For example, other people may be affected by my conduct because they dislike it, find it disgusting, or regard it as immoral. These effects, taken in themselves, are never good reasons for interfering with my conduct. In thus ignoring certain effects, Mill's defence of liberty is not utilitarian. A utilitarian cannot disregard any of the effects of my conduct since they are all part of its consequences, and help to determine whether the suppression of my conduct or leaving me free will maximize happiness. Various attempts to show that a sophisticated utilitarian can consistently discount certain pleasures and pains, or the satisfaction or frustration of certain desires, are considered and rejected.

Recent studies of Mill suggest that his version of the principle or utility is not a moral principle but a principle for evaluating all conduct, both moral and non-moral. On this view, only conduct which breaches moral standards can be subjected to sanctions or punishment by society. On the other hand, a person's faults in the self-regarding sphere are not properly regarded as immoral, and so should not be interfered with. It is argued that Mill's moral theory, being only a branch of his principle of utility, does not always require us to act to maximize happiness. Some acts which fail to maximize happiness are not morally wrong. In Chapter 3 I provide some background to the understanding of these recent studies, and I then examine one such interpretation of the limited scope of Mill's moral theory. I argue that if there is a conflict between the maximization of happiness and some moral requirement, a consistent utilitarian would have to resolve it in favour of the former. He cannot allow moral considerations to override non-moral ones. On the other hand, there may be no possibility of a conflict between moral and non-moral appraisals because morally required acts are a sub-class of acts which maximize happiness. But assuming again that self-regarding conduct does not belong to the moral realm, it does not follow that such conduct is immune from the application of sanctions. For a utilitarian sanctions are applicable whenever it will maximize happiness to apply them, irrespective of whether the conduct to which sanctions are applied is morally right or wrong or even non-moral. So if Mill is still a utilitarian, even though his moral theory is restricted in scope, then the area of application of sanctions cannot be confined in principle to the moral sphere. Hiving off self-regarding conduct to a non-moral realm does not guarantee that on utilitarian grounds it should never be interfered with.

Mill's liberty principle states that the only purpose for which interference with the conduct of individuals is permitted is to 'prevent harm to others'. In Chapter 4 I suggest that Mill's notion of harm is narrower than that which a consistent utilitarian would accept. The basis of it is the idea of infringing the rules which are necessary for the viability of any society, but Mill complicates the notion in several ways. I then discuss the range of conduct that Mill brings within the scope of his formula that justifiable interference with the conduct of individuals must 'prevent harm to others'.

In Chapter 5 I analyse Mill's ideal of individuality which lies at the basis of his defence of freedom of action and freedom of discussion. Freedom is an ingredient of individuality in that individuality consists partly in choosing freely and critically between alternative beliefs and activities or plans of life. But the content of the choice is also important. It should be such as to develop certain distinctive human capacities and powers, as well as each person's special potentialities. I also discuss the connection between happiness and individuality, and argue that Mill's plea for individuality cannot be usefully described as utilitarian. The chapter ends with an examination of the extent to which Mill's doctrine of individuality is consistent with a belief in objective truths.

In his liberty principle Mill highlights certain bad reasons for interfering with a person's conduct: 'He cannot rightfully be compelled to do or forbear because it will be better for him to do so, because it will make him happier, because in the opinions of others, to do so would be wise, or even right.' Mill strongly rejects paternalism and the enforcement of the dominant shared values of a society. For this he has been severely criticized. In Chaper 6 I show that Mill recognized the function of shared values in promoting social stability, and that his view here is consistent with the importance he attached to individual liberty. Chapter 7 is devoted to a discussion of different versions of paternalism and different justifications of it. Particular emphasis is given to some of Mill's examples, and to the implications of changes in a person's attitude towards his past conduct.

In Chapter 8 I turn to Mill's defence of freedom of expression. This is the subject of the longest, and for many the finest, chapter in *On Liberty*. I distinguish between different types of argument presented by Mill, and show that he attaches the greatest significance to the manner in which a person holds his beliefs in the important areas of 'morals, religion, politics, social relations, and the business of life'. The chapter also examines the sorts of restrictions on freedom of expression that are compatible with Mill's arguments. I claim that though there are grounds for restricting the circumstances in which blasphemous, obscene, and racist remarks may be expressed, they should not be suppressed simply because they offend some people, be they a small minority or even the overwhelming majority.

In the final chapter I consider some unusual attacks on Mill's essay. It is generally accepted, both by Mill's supporters and by his critics, that *On Liberty* is a passionate defence of the liberty of every group in society and not just of the privileged few. But recently it is claimed that Mill's liberalism is really a defence of the liberty of the 'the superior few', and that he was intolerant of the others towards whom he showed signs of 'moral totalitarianism'. It is also argued from another quarter that although *On Liberty* is a liberal tract defending the liberty of individuals generally, it is inconsistent with most of Mill's other works. The views that are supposed to be expressed in these other works are then used to attack the Mill of *On Liberty*, so that we are presented with a picture of 'the two Mills' with the Mill of *On Liberty* as the clear villain. Chapter 9 is a defence of Mill from both these attacks.

In this book I have tried to show that Mill's case for liberty is not wholly reconcilable with any consistent version of utilitarianism. I do not thereby suggest that Mill is an inconsistent thinker. On the whole, *On Liberty* is both internally consistent and also consistent with nearly all of Mill's other writings. But it is as a consistent liberal, deeply committed to the cause of individual freedom for everyone, that Mill should be remembered.

2

Self-Regarding Conduct

I. THE TRADITIONAL INTERPRETATION

What is the nature and basis of Mill's distinction between self- and other-regarding conduct? According to the traditional interpretation, self-regarding actions have no effect on others against their wishes; they only affect the agents and consenting adults. This interpretation has provided much of the basis for the criticism of Mill's allegedly false individualism which sees society merely as a collection of atomistic individuals, each one capable of living in substantial independence of the others.[1] As against this, Mill's critics remind us that man lives in a society, and he is not, and cannot be, isolated from others. Except for a few very trivial actions which no one has ever thought of suppressing, all our actions will affect others in some way. This will be readily seen if we think not just of the physical effects on others such as are produced by being punched, stabbed, or shot at, but also of the mental anguish and suffering produced. As Robert Paul Wolff points out, to a devout Calvinist or a principled vegetarian the 'very presence in his community of a Catholic or a meat-eater may cause him fully as much pain as a blow to the face or the theft of his purse'.[2] There are therefore no self-regarding actions of any importance, and in setting up a protective fence around such actions, Mill only succeeded in defending the freedom of individuals to engage in trivial activities. But whenever an act provokes the anger, resentment, or disgust of others, it clearly affects them and thus falls into the category of other-regarding conduct.

In defending Mill's notion of self-regarding conduct, his disciple Morley maintained that we should set a limit to what may properly be considered as the effects of an act such that the remote effects on others should not be counted.[3] Morley also claimed that it is unreasonable to bring in the 'indirect and negative consequences' of the act which consist in the agent's neglect of some socially useful activities while he is performing an act which otherwise affects only himself.[4] But these restrictions on what are to count as the effects of an act are insufficient to show that there are non-trivial acts which have no effect on others. For acts which are disliked, abhorred, or viewed with repugnance by others, all affect them immediately and positively. Yet it is clear that Mill would not count such effects as disqualifying an act from membership of the self-regarding class.

Mill readily and explicitly admits that self-regarding conduct affects others, and this admission is fatal to the traditional interpretation. Thus he acknowledges that 'the mischief which a person does to himself may seriously affect, both through their sympathies and their interests, those nearly connected with him and, in a minor degree, society at large' (p. 137). He also writes that a person's self-regarding conduct which affects him directly, 'may affect others through himself' (p. 75).

II. AFFECTING THE INTERESTS OF OTHERS

In his important paper 'A Re-Reading of Mill on Liberty',[5] J. C. Rees very effectively criticizes the traditional interpretation and provides an alternative interpretation. Rees maintains that self-regarding actions do not affect the interests of others. He claims that there is for Mill a distinction between merely 'affecting others' and affecting the interests of others', and that in some crucial passages when he is stating his principle, Mill uses the notion of interests rather than that of effects. To say that somebody's conduct affects others is to make a factual statement, whereas to claim that a person's interests are affected is to make a statement that is in part normative. Whether one's interests are affected depends on whether one is affected in a way that is regarded as important. We appeal to certain standards or values in determining whether interests have been affected. On the other hand, a person can be affected by an act simply because he is extrasensitive. The peculiarities of one's tastes, and other subjective factors, can determine whether one is affected by another's conduct. But whether or not interests are affected does not depend on such factors. There is an objective element in the notion of interests such that not just any effect will count as an effect on interests.

Rees also argues that the notion of interests is different from that of effects because Mill links interests to the notion of rights. Thus Mill says that individuals should not injure the interests of one another, 'or rather certain interests which, either by express provision or by tacit understanding, ought to be considered as rights' (p. 132). This link between interests and rights again shows that standards and values are invoked when one claims that interests are violated in the way that they are not when one talks of effects.

According to Rees, interests 'depend for their existence on social recognition and are closely connected with prevailing standards about the sort of behaviour a man can legitimately expect from others'.[6] But if this is the case, then the area of individual liberty is to a large extent determined by prevailing standards and values. Now Mill, when he put forward his principle, was concerned to set a barrier against the tryranny of the majority. But on Rees's account his principle would strengthen the hands of the majority. For it follows that the extent to which the conduct of the individual may be interfered with now depends on what are recognized by prevailing standards as the individual's interests. It is therefore the values of the majority which determine whether or not other people's interests are violated by a person's conduct, and hence whether his conduct falls within the area of legitimate intervention by law and public opinion. But since Mill feared so much the tyranny of prevailing values, and explicitly fought against it, it seems highly unlikely that he would subscribe to a notion of self-regarding conduct that places individuals at the mercy of these values. As Wollheim has argued, Rees's interpretation makes Mill's principle both conservative and relativistic in its application.[7] It is conservative because the area of individual liberty will only be enlarged with difficulty since there must first be a favourable change in socially recognized norms. The principle is also relativistic because its content will vary greatly from one society to another, depending on what the respective prevailing norms are.

If the appeal to prevailing standards will not do, perhaps

it is possible to give another account of interests which makes it dependent on a more acceptable set of standards and values. Since Mill explicitly professes to be a utilitarian of some sort, it is tempting to explicate interests in terms of the principle of utility. Such an account has been offered by Ted Honderich.[8] He agrees with Rees that there is a distinction between interests and effects, but disagrees about the nature of the relevant interests. Self-regarding actions are those actions which do not violate what *ought* to be the interests of others, and the standard of what ought to be the interests of others is provided by the principle of utility. The relevant interests are therefore no longer determined by the variable and varying prevailing standards of different societies, and Mill's principle is rescued from conservatism and relativism.

There are, however, difficulties in Honderich's account that he himself lucidly and candidly explores. For a utilitarian, Mill's liberty principle would be secondary or subordinate to the principle of utility. Its status should be similar to that of other secondary principles, like the principles that one should keep one's promises and that one should tell the truth. These secondary principles give more detailed and precise guides than does the principle of utility itself as to how one should act on particular occasions. But they are secondary in the sense that they derive their justification from the ultimate principle of utility: keeping one's promises and telling the truth will maximize happiness at least in most cases. A secondary principle is therefore something *distinct* from the principle of utility, but justifiable in terms of it. However, on Honderich's account Mill's principle is not distinct from the principle of utility. For self-regarding actions do not violate what ought to be the interests of others, and 'what ought to be in the interests of others' is defined in terms of the principle of utility. The principle of utility enters into the very formulation of Mill's allegedly secondary principle. It would therefore have been simpler if Mill had defended liberty by directly applying the principle of utility instead of proceeding via the liberty principle. For, on this view, the liberty principle cannot in any case be stated without reference to the principle of utility.

There is a general objection to any account of self-regarding conduct that depends on making a distinction between interests and effects. Mill does not seem to recognize any such distinction.[9] It is of course true that the term 'interests' is often used in stating his principle. But he also uses a host of other expressions, especially 'what affects others' and 'what concerns others', and he moves easily from one expression to another in a way which suggests that he is using the terms 'interests', 'effects', and 'concerns' interchangeably. Indeed, just as he allows that self-regarding actions may affect others, he too concedes that they may affect indirectly the interests of others: 'But there is a sphere of action in which society, as distinguished from the individual, has, if any, only an indirect interest; . . .' (p. 75). He goes on to acknowledge the possible effects on others of self-regarding conduct. The important distinction for him is not that between interests and effects, but rather that between direct and indirect interests, or, what amounts to the same thing, direct and indirect effects. Elsewhere in the essay, as Rees points out, Mill uses similar phrases to draw the line between self- and other-regarding conduct. The contrast is between what _primarily_ and _chiefly_ concerns the interests of the individual, and what primarily or chiefly concerns the interests of society.[10]

The ultimate importance of Rees's interpretation does not depend on there being a distinction between interests and effects, for what he has shown is that Mill wanted to distinguish between the different types of effects that an action may have. Rees has decisively refuted the traditional interpretation, and he has established that self-regarding conduct affects others in certain ways. So the problem now is to give a coherent account of the nature of the effects on others that self-regarding conduct may have.

III. THE IRRELEVANCE OF SOCIETY'S 'LIKINGS AND DISLIKINGS'

According to Mill, an action indirectly affects others, or the interests of others, if it affects them simply because they dislike it, or find it repugnant or immoral. Soon after stating his principle, he picks out three areas of self-regarding conduct. The difference between other-regarding and self-regarding actions in the area of 'tastes and pursuits' is expressed in terms of actions which 'harm' our fellow creatures on the one hand, and on the other hand, actions which do not harm them 'even though they should think our conduct foolish, perverse or wrong'. Again, before he states his liberty principle, he considers certain attitudes which he thinks have worked against the cause of freedom. He criticizes those who 'have occupied themselves rather in inquiring what things society ought to like or dislike, than in questioning whether their likings or dislikings should be a law to individuals' (pp. 70–1). His principle is meant to oppose such attitudes.

Sometimes the feelings of abhorrence and dislike can be very intense, and in this way self-regarding conduct can seriously affect others. But Mill deplores a state of affairs in which punishment and severe social pressures are brought to bear on actions which merely arouse society's intense dislike and repugnance. He points out that 'wherever the sentiment of the majority is still genuine and intense, it is found to have abated little of its claim to be obeyed.' (p. 71.) We have such a situation if a society, consisting of a majority of Muslims, prohibited the eating of pork. Mill reminds us that they find the practice 'really revolting' and they 'also sincerely think that it is forbidden and abhorred by the Deity' (p. 142). The only tenable ground we can have for condemning such a prohibition is that 'with the personal tastes and self-regarding concerns of individuals the public has no business to interfere.' In other words, only by adopting the liberty principle can we have a reason for ruling out the appeal to the majority's genuine feelings of repugnance and revulsion as a ground for interfering with individual liberty. Mill's essay *On Liberty* is a protest against the appeal, which he felt was so often made, to such feelings of the majority as relevant and good reasons for restricting the actions of individuals. According to him they are in themselves never relevant or good reasons for interference. If the only reason that can be given for wishing to restrict an individual's action is an appeal to such feelings, or to the mere belief that the conduct is wrong, then the individual's action is a self-regarding one. If however the action harms others, or violates 'a distinct and assignable obligation', then an additional factor is introduced which takes it out of the self-regarding into the other-regarding class. But even so Mill insists that we should give the proper reason for intervention:

If, for example, a man, through intemperance or extravagance, becomes unable to pay his debts, or having undertaken the moral responsibility of a family, becomes from some cause incapable of supporting or educating them, he is deservedly reprobated, and might be justly punished; but it is for the breach of duty to his family or creditors, not for the extravagance. (p. 138.)

Mill wants to revise the framework within which questions about individual liberty and society's right of interference are raised and answered. A principled defence of individual liberty will reject the idea that the 'likings and dislikings' of society shall dictate what individuals are permitted to do. But such a defence has generally not been given. It is only in the area of religious belief that 'the higher ground has been taken on principle and maintained with consistency, by any but an individual here and there' (p. 71). But even here religious toleration has only been practically realized when there is religious indifference. 'Wherever the sentiment of the majority is still genuine and intense, it is found to have abated little of its claim to be obeyed.' (p. 71.) We would certainly think it unjust if we were in the minority and a majority, because it strongly disapproved of our religious practices, prohibited them. By the same token, we should recognize that we ourselves have no better case for prohibiting anything simply because we find it offensive and we are in the majority. We should not adopt 'the logic of persecutors' and claim that 'we may persecute others because we are right, and that they must not persecute us because they are wrong' (p. 142). His liberty principle provides the basis for our consistently excluding all such cases of oppression by the majority.

Mill wants to show that a consistent defence of individual liberty will involve the application of his liberty principle not just to religious beliefs and practices, where it has already a limited acceptance, but also to all other similar cases. The adoption of his principle excludes the use of a certain kind of balancing as the basis for interference with liberty. The outraged sensibilities of the majority are not to be weighed against the feelings of those whose conduct offends the majority. The mere fact that one is offended by the conduct of others carries no weight.

There are many who consider as an injury to themselves any conduct which they have a distaste for, and resent it as an outrage to their feelings; as a religious bigot, when charged with disregarding the religious feelings of others, has been known to retort that they disregard his feelings, by persisting in their abominable worship or creed. But there is no parity between the feeling of a person for his own opinion, and the feeling of another who is offended at his holding it; no more than between the desire of a thief to take a purse, and the desire of the right owner to keep it. And a person's taste is as much his own peculiar concern as his opinion or his purse. (p. 140.)

Mill says that his case for liberty is not based on 'the idea of abstract right, as a thing independent of utility'. By this he means that he is not simply going to intuit the value of liberty, or baldly and boldly to assert its value without further argument. He is going to base his case on 'utility in the largest sense'. Now it appears that part of his argument for liberty rests on spelling out the different implications of accepting or rejecting his liberty principle. The rejection of his principle will have undesirable consequences in that it will lead to religious intolerance. He focuses on religious examples because here the undesirable consequences or implications of the rejection of his principle will be appreciated with less difficulty by more people. But he generalizes from particular cases and tries to show that any sound and consistent defence of religious toleration will lead to the acceptance of his principle, and therefore to the recognition of a wider area of individual freedom.

In giving a unified account of the value of promoting freedom with respect to self-regarding conduct generally, Mill also appeals to the different types of benefit that freedom brings to society and to the agents themselves. Some of these benefits are the effects of freedom. Thus he points out that freedom will allow individuals to conduct 'experiments in living', and to learn from their own and other people's experiences and mistakes. In this way people are more likely to discover enjoyable and worthwhile activities. In *Utilitarianism* he remarks that a 'cultivated mind' will find 'sources of inexhaustible interest in all that surrounds it; in the objects of nature, the achievements of art, the imaginations of poetry, the incidents of history, the ways of mankind, past and present, and their prospects in the future.'[11] Any ordinary

person in 'a civilized country' can aquire the requisite amount
of 'mental culture'. Mill regards the absence of freedom as
one of the principal barriers to the attainment of human
happiness.

In a world in which there is so much to interest, so much to enjoy, and
so much also to correct and improve, everyone who has this moderate
amount of moral and intellectual requisites is capable of an existence
which may be called enviable; and unless such a person, through bad
laws, or subjection to the will of others, is denied the liberty to use the
sources of happiness within his reach, he will not fail to find this
enviable existence, if he escape the positive evils of life, the great
sources of physical and mental suffering — such as indigence, disease,
and the unkindness, worthlessness, or premature loss of objects of
affection.[12]

However, the relation between freedom and some of its
benefits is not properly described in terms of cause and
effect, means and end. Mill regards freedom as important
for individuals to form and to develop their 'characters', to
express themselves both in words and in deeds, to cultivate
what he calls 'the free development of individuality'. His
ideal of individuality will be examined in detail in Chapter
5, but at present it is enough to note that freedom is an
ingredient of individuality rather than a mere means to its
promotion. Freedom is a component of Mill's view of a
desirable form of life and of the happiness associated with
such a life.

In treating as irrelevant the repugnance and abhorrence of
the majority towards some self-regarding actions, Mill goes
against the classical utilitarian's view that all pleasures and
pains are relevant in determining the rightness or wrongness
of an act. Mill's view also seems to be inconsistent with
preference utilitarianism which regards the satisfaction of
any desire as in itself good. The frustration of people's desire
to suppress self-regarding conduct carries no weight. But can
a consistent utilitarian discount, as Mill evidently wants to,
the adverse effects on others that are produced by some
self-regarding actions? This is the question to which we shall
now turn.

IV. UTILITARIANISM AND SELF-REGARDING
CONDUCT: WOLLHEIM'S INTERPRETATION

In a recent paper entitled 'John Stuart Mill and the Limits of State Action' Richard Wollheim gives a subtle and comprehensive account of Mill's notion of self-regarding actions.[13] According to Wollheim, self-regarding actions are 'those actions which affect either the agent alone or other people solely insofar as they believe such actions to be right or wrong' (p. 9). Although, as we shall see at the end of this section, Wollheim omits some acts that Mill would wish to include in the self-regarding category, his account of what Mill means by such acts is substantially correct. However, he fails in his ingenious attempt to reconcile his interpretation of self-regarding actions with utilitarianism. He does not succeed in showing that Millian liberalism, as embodied in the claim that there are never good reasons for prohibiting self-regarding actions, is compatible with utilitarianism.

Wollheim points out that at first sight there may appear to be a conflict between his account of self-regarding conduct and the utilitarian doctrine. This is because, on Wollheim's interpretation, Mill is committed to disregarding as irrelevant the pain or distress of outraged moral and religious sensibilities. But a utilitarian must surely take into account any pain produced by an act. Rawls has given a vivid illustration. Suppose that the majority in a society has such an intense abhorrence for certain religious or sexual practices that even the very thought that these practices are going on in private and out of their view is enough to arouse anger and hatred.

Seeking the greatest satisfaction of desire may, then, justify harsh repressive measures against actions that cause no social injury. To defend individual liberty in this case the utilitarian has to show that given the circumstances the real balance of advantages in the long run still lies on the side of freedom; and this argument may or may not be successful.[14]

However, Wollheim uses two arguments to show that the utilitarian is ultimately justified in ignoring the pain caused solely by the belief that an action is wrong. If these two arguments succeed, then the utilitarian does not have to go in for the kind of balancing of pleasures and pains that Rawls suggests.

I shall begin with the second argument. Wollheim maintains

that Mill has two criteria for distinguishing a preference from
a moral belief. First, a preference is based on feelings and
emotions. It is not supported by reasons, and according to
Wollheim, Mill was only prepared to accept reasons which
appealed to the consequences of the act. The second criterion
is that a preference is personal in the sense that it is not about
how others ought to behave, but only about the individual's
own conduct.

Wollheim points out that many, though not all, of the
beliefs in question are mere preferences according to the first
criterion. The beliefs we are considering are those which
condemn actions as wrong even though these actions cause
no harm or pain to others independently of their being
thought wrong. Since the actions cause no independent harm,
no reason of the relevant utilitarian kind can be given to
show that they are wrong. Hence the belief that they are
wrong must be a preference by the first criterion. We cannot,
for example, say that a self-regarding action is wrong because
it pains others, for the pain does not exist independently of
the belief that the conduct is wrong, and hence cannot be
cited in support of it. However, Wollheim shows that there
are some beliefs of the type in question which are not preferences. In these cases the actions condemned by the beliefs
also cause no independent harm, but it is genuinely believed
that they cause such harm, and this sincere, though mistaken,
belief is the reason for the condemnation. Wollheim gives the
example of someone who believes that smoking marijuana
causes impotence, and this belief is his reason for supporting
the legal penalties against marijuana smoking. His belief,
then, is not a preference according to the first criterion,
because the belief is supported by a reason which appeals to
the consequences of the act.

The next step in Wollheim's argument is to show that for
Mill the two criteria for preferences are linked in that if a
belief is a preference by the first criterion, then it will also
satisfy the second criterion. He argues that in *Utilitarianism*
Mill holds the view that a judgement can only be considered
a moral judgement if it is based on an appeal to consequences.
If, in justifying his act, an agent is not prepared to give a
reason which invokes the consequences of the act, then his

judgement on the act is not a moral judgement. But the agent who cannot back his judgement with relevant reasons has merely stated his preference, according to the first criterion of a preference. But, at the same time, the judgement is also not a moral belief about what all should or ought to do in similar situations. So what is the nature of the judgement? Wollheim concludes that Mill would seem to have only one answer: it is a judgement of personal taste or inclination about what the agent himself should do, and hence it satisfies the second criterion of a preference. If this linkage between the two criteria for preferences is granted, then the rest of Wollheim's argument can proceed.

Suppose X is a self-regarding action which 'causes' pain to another person simply because he believes X to be wrong. Since this belief is not supported by a utilitarian reason, it is a preference according to the first criterion. But, because of the linkage between the two criteria for preferences, the belief will also satisfy the second criterion for a preference. From this, it follows that the belief cannot be about the conduct of others. For according to the second criterion for a preference, a preference only refers to what the person who has the preference would like to be or to do. So X cannot really violate his preference since X is the conduct of another agent. The pain that the person experiences when he sees, or comtemplates, someone else's performance of X cannot therefore be attributed to X. He is mistaken in thinking that X is the cause of his pain. Since X causes no other pain, there is no utilitarian reason for interfering with it.

The person who thinks that X is the cause of his pain in fact mistakes his preference for a moral belief. For example, he thinks that he holds the moral belief that homosexuality is wrong, and that is why the homosexual acts of others distress him. In fact his belief, being a preference, relates only to his own conduct. Perhaps he believes that a homosexual life is not the life *he* would like to lead. Wollheim suggests that the association in his mind between his pain and the homosexual acts arises very likely from his own desires and fears about homosexuality. Perhaps he himself both desires to indulge in homosexual acts, and is afraid to do so.

However, Wollheim's attempt to link the two criteria for

preferences fails. The linkage exists only when an *agent* is making a judgement about his *own* conduct. But of course we make judgements not only when we are agents, but also when we are spectators. In the case of a judgement about other people's conduct, from the fact that it is not a moral judgement but a preference according to the first criterion, it cannot be inferred that it is also a preference according to the second criterion. For my judgement may be personal in one of Wollheim's senses, in the sense that it stems from my own feelings and emotions, and yet not be personal in the required sense that it relates only to my conduct. My feelings and emotions may be related to the conduct of others. So the link between the two criteria for preferences is present only in the case of a person's judgements on his own conduct. But in the context of self-regarding conduct, it is our judgements on other people's self-regarding conduct, and not on our own, that raise a problem for the utilitarian.

Certainly Wollheim is right in drawing attention to the importance for Mill of the distinction between a preference and a moral belief. But there is no evidence that Mill accepted the second criterion for a preference. In a long footnote to his edition of his father's *Analysis of the Phenomena of the Human Mind*, Mill states the distinction between a moral belief and a preference:

> This strong association of the idea of punishment and the desire for its infliction, with the idea of the act which has hurt us, is not in itself a moral sentiment, but it appears to me to be the element which is present when we have the feelings of obligation and of injury, and which mainly distinguishes them from simple distaste and dislike for anything *in the conduct of another* that is disagreeable to us, that distinguishes, for instance, our feeling towards the person who steals our goods, from our feeling towards him who offends our senses by smoking tobacco.[15] *(My italics.)*

Here is an explicit statement that a preference, or a 'simple distaste or dislike', can be about 'the conduct of another', such as his smoking tobacco. The same view is also expressed in Mill's essay on Bentham, where he speaks of liking or disliking other people's conduct which 'neither does good nor harm', as opposed to having the moral sentiments of approval or disapproval.[16] Again there is not the slightest hint that preferences are to be restricted in scope to the conduct of the person who has the preference.

With these two passages from Mill's other works in mind, we can return to the essay *On Liberty* and see whether there is anything there which suggests a different account of the nature of preferences. But, curiously, the only passage cited by Wollheim which bears on the scope of a preference goes *against* his account. For in it, as Wollheim himself acknowledges, Mill refers to the existence of preferences about what others should do: specifically, Mill mentions a religious bigot's distaste for the religious beliefs and practices of others.[17] Wollheim treats this remark as an aberration from Mill's main characterization of preferences as limited in scope to the conduct of the person having the preference. But the belief that preferences can be about the conduct of others is, as we have seen, very much in line with Mill's comments elsewhere, and far from being an isolated remark, it seems to be part of his considered view of the nature of preferences.

But if preferences can refer to the conduct of others, then Wollheim's argument collapses. For the admission that a belief is a preference does not imply that another person's conduct will not violate it. So a self-regarding act can violate other people's preferences, and can therefore cause them pain. Without further argument a utilitarian would not be justified in placing it completely outside the scope of social intervention.

I now turn to Wollheim's first argument. This can be divided into two parts. The first part of the argument is that if the only effect an action has on others is through their belief that the action is wrong, then the belief in question must be false. This is because the utilitarian calculation of the pleasures and pains caused by an action must be made as if in a world prior to the adoption of moral attitudes. Otherwise one would have to include the pleasures and pains caused by the action through various moral beliefs. And if these pleasures and pains are included, then the rightness or wrongness of an action will, to some extent, be determined by whether people feel or believe the action to be right or wrong. If, for example, people feel strongly enough that a particular action is wrong, and they are severely distressed by the mere contemplation of the action, then these pains may be bad enough to make the action wrong. So if one counts the pleasures and pains caused by various moral beliefs, then it is possible for an action to be right or wrong simply because a sufficient number of people *feel* strongly enough that the action is right or wrong. But this is absurd. If one now disregards the pain which arises simply from the belief that an action is wrong, then a self-regarding action has no painful consequences, and hence cannot be wrong on utilitarian grounds. The belief that it is wrong must therefore be a false belief.

Having established that the beliefs in question are false, Wollheim enters the second part of his argument by asking: why should the utilitarian Mill ignore the pain caused by the false beliefs about an action? After all, these pains are no less real than the pains arising from true beliefs. Wollheim says that Mill was perhaps inclined simply to disregard the pain caused through false beliefs in the same way that he looked down on the comforts of unreason and error. This inclination is supported by Mill's view that as intellectual inquiry progresses, false moral beliefs will be eliminated.

However, these considerations only show Mill to be a very imperfect utilitarian, and this goes against Wollheim's general thesis. Perhaps Mill is right that false moral beliefs will vanish with the progress of intellectual inquiry, but a good utilitarian will still take into account the pain brought about by false beliefs so long as the pain exists. Of course if he thinks that certain false beliefs will soon disappear he will not give much significance to the distress to which they give rise. But here what discounts the distress is not the *falsity* of the beliefs, but the short-lived or temporary nature of the distress. And if Mill was disposed bluntly to discount both the pleasures and pains arising from false beliefs as such, then he would have abandoned the utilitarian axiom that all pleasures as such are good, and all pains as such are evil.

However, even though in the second part of his argument Wollheim does not succeed in explaining why a utilitarian would ignore the pain caused through false beliefs, there was no need for him to have embarked on this task. The first part of his argument, if sound, already gives him all that is necessary. For he has already explained why the pain caused by the belief that the act is wrong should be ignored: it is because otherwise an act can be made wrong simply by a sufficient number of people feeling strongly enough that it is wrong. But if *any* pain so caused may be disregarded, then of course it follows that any pain caused by a *false* belief about the wrongness of the act may be ignored. No additional argument is needed. However, what is crucial to Wollheim's argument here is not the fact that the belief is false, but rather the fact that the belief is one concerning the *morality* of the act. As Wollheim maintains, the utilitarian calculation must be made prior to the adoption of moral attitudes. The distress in question is to be ignored not because it stems from a false belief, but rather because it stems from a belief about the morality of the act. In a different case, a person may hold the false belief that someone is going to kill him, and as a result live in constant fear and trembling. The distress caused by this kind of false belief must be taken into account by the utilitarian, and nothing that Wollheim has said shows otherwise. But this is not the kind of distress caused by self-regarding conduct. A self-regarding action causes no relevant pain because the only pain it causes arises from the belief that it is wrong, and this pain, we have seen, is to be ignored. So it does seem that, in most cases, there would be no utilitarian reason for interfering with such actions.

However, I add the qualification 'in most cases' because some self-regarding actions may cause harm to the agent himself, either immediately or in the future. And given that the harm is bad enough, there will be a good utilitarian reason for paternalistic intervention to prevent the agent from harming himself. So further argument is needed to show why the utilitarian would reject paternalism. But this qualification aside, the first part of Wollheim's argument, if sound, would appear to show that there is no utilitarian basis for interfering with self-regarding conduct. But his argument is unsound.

Wollheim maintains that the utilitarian must disregard the

pleasures and pains which arise simply from the adoption of moral attitudes towards an action, for otherwise the morality of the action will, in certain circumstances, be crucially determined by the mere strength of people's feelings about its rightness or wrongness. But this argument, as elaborated by Wollheim, suffers a little from an ambiguity in the scope of the pleasures and pains that are to be ruled out by the utilitarian. In one place Wollheim refers to 'pleasurable and unpleasurable moral responses', and here what are pleasurable and unpleasurable respectively are the favourable and unfavorable moral responses themselves. But Wollheim also refers to a causal connection between the pleasures and pains on the one hand, and the associated moral beliefs on the other hand. And in general he refers to the effects on others of self-regarding actions as effects which proceed only 'via certain beliefs they hold' (p. 8), or as effects which are brought about 'solely insofar as they believe such actions to be right or wrong' (p. 9). But the extent of the effects on others that self-regarding actions can have will depend on whether or not we are to include among such effects all those caused by the beliefs these people hold about the morality of the actions. For example, it may be part of being a sincere and committed Sabbatarian that one is distressed, to some extent at least, by the licensing of Sunday entertainments. But different Sabbatarians will be distressed to different degreees. Suppose that some are so distressed that they are physically ill. Such illness is causally linked to their beliefs about the wrongness of Sunday entertainments. Is the physical illness therefore to be considered a part of the effects of Sunday entertainments? Or do we, as Wollheim seems to suggest on one occasion (pp. 12–13), confine the relevant effects to the mental anguish that the contemplation of the act causes in those who think it wrong?

However, there are several arguments that the utilitarian may use to try to show that, in spite of the harm in question, self-regarding conduct should never be interfered with. The first argument is to deny that the harm — the serious illness of the morally sensitive person — is to be attributed to the self-regarding conduct of others. In other words, it is not the violations of his moral beliefs which give rise to the harm.

The cause of the harm is the person's own peculiar personality. A normal person, who holds the same moral views, will not be as seriously affected as this sensitive person is by the mere awareness that others are committing immoral acts. The difference must therefore be attributed, not to these acts, but to the person's unusual, and indeed, extreme sensitivity. It is this extreme sensitivity which is the real cause of his illness.[18]

But the argument, so far, does not provide the utilitarian with a reason for never prohibiting self-regarding acts. For granted that such acts do not cause the illness, it remains true that the acts are causally relevant in the production of the illness. What the utilitarian needs to show is that such a prohibition is never the most economical or effective way of preventing the illness, or that the cost in utilitarian terms of such prohibition will always outweigh the evil of the illness. These he may or may not be able to show. For example, it may be relatively easy to shield a sensitive person from the knowledge that sexual immoralities are committed every night in his society, or to steel him to face such knowledge with calmness. But if it proves to be impossible to do either, the utilitarian could still plausibly argue that it is better for the sensitive person to be seriously ill rather than for the state to prohibit all the self-regarding actions which will offend his moral sensibilities. The cost in terms of human misery, and limited police resources, of such prohibitions will considerably outweigh the evil of one person's serious illness. However, all that the argument attempts to show is that the harm is not *sufficient* to justify the suppression of self-regarding actions. But the harm must *always* be taken into account in any utilitarian calculation of whether certain self-regarding actions should be permitted.

But I have still not come to grips with Wollheim's argument that 'the Utilitarian calculation must be made as if in a world prior to the adoption of moral attitudes.' (p. 12.) His argument here fails to make a couple of distinctions. First, it is necessary to distinguish between those pleasures and pains which arise from the adoption of *utilitarian* moral attitudes, and those pleasures and pains which arise from the adoption of *non*-utilitarian moral attitudes. Prior to the adoption of any moral attitude, a self-regarding action causes no pain to others, and once again, leaving aside the effect on the agent himself, there is no utilitarian basis for believing it to be wrong. Hence if a utilitarian, who is aware of this fact, still regards the action as wrong, and it thereby distressed by it, then there is something irrational about him. But from the non-utilitarian point of view, the action may properly be regarded as wrong even though it has no undesirable consequences independently of its being so regarded. For the ground of the moral judgement that the act is wrong may have nothing to do with the consequences of the act. This point is of some significance because most of those who are likely to be distressed as a result of their beliefs about the wrongness of some self-regarding actions will be non-utilitarians. Now, the distress of *non*-utilitarians can be treated as something that occurs prior to the *utilitarian* moral judgement on a self-regarding action. This being the case, there is no reason why the utilitarian should ignore the distress. The distress occurs prior to the adoption of utilitarian moral attitudes, and therefore constitutes part of the data which the utilitarian has to take into account before he decides on the morality of the action. So even a self-regarding action can be wrong if it causes enough distress to non-utilitarians.

But now, suppose I am wrong about this, and the distress of the non-utilitarian may be ignored by the utilitarian. It follows, then, that no self-regarding act is morally wrong from the utilitarian point of view. But it does not follow that, on utilitarian grounds, it would always be wrong legally to prohibit such acts, or to punish persons for engaging in them. This is because punishing an act X is itself an act that is distinct from X, and may have consequences different from the consequences of X. This distinction is of course analogous to that between the morality of an act and the morality of praising or condemning a person for performing that act, a distinction that utilitarians themselves have emphasized.[19] Now armed with this distinction, we can accept Wollheim's claim that 'the Utilitarian calculation must be made as if in a world prior to the adoption of moral attitudes', and yet reject his unqualified view that the utilitarian may ignore the distress which arises by way of the belief that a self-regarding act is wrong. For now there are different levels from which the distress may be viewed. With respect to the morality of X, we are to ignore the distress which proceeds from the belief that X is wrong. But if the question concerns the morality of punishing or prohibiting X, then the distress produced by the belief that X is wrong *is* relevant to the utilitarian calculation. For though the distress does not exist prior to the adoption of moral attitudes about X, it exists prior to the adoption of moral attitudes about the punishment or prohibition of X.

I conclude therefore that Wollheim does not succeed in reconciling Mill's defence of self-regarding conduct with utilitarianism. Moreover, any attempt at reconciliation will have to face an additional difficulty because Wollheim's account of self-regarding conduct is defective in at least one respect. He says that if there are actions that produce 'immediate revulsion or disgust', then these actions are not self-regarding. This is because, on his account, self-regarding conduct affects others only in so far as they believe the conduct to be wrong. But the immediate revulsion or disgust is independent of any belief about the wrongness of the acts in question. Wollheim is right that the utilitarian would have to include such immediate revulsion and disgust in his calculation. But this places the utilitarian even further away from Mill. For it seems quite obvious that Mill would not regard the revulsion or disgust as a relevant reason for interfering with self-regarding conduct. In the essay he attacks those who tried to regulate the conduct of others simply on the basis of their feelings, their mere likes and dislikes, and he argues against the imposition on others not only of one's opinions or beliefs, but also of one's inclinations. Wollheim's exclusion of conduct which arouses immediate revulsion or disgust has the following odd consequence. A person who is immediately disgusted with another's conduct, and who can give no reason at all for his disgust, can none the less rightly claim that his disgust is to be taken into account by the utilitarian. But, on the other hand, Wollheim would allow the utilitarian to ignore the same person's disgust if it is based on a deeply held, and even clearly articulated, non-utilitarian moral belief about the wrongness of the act.

V. DWORKIN ON EXTERNAL PREFERENCES

In his book *Taking Rights Seriously*, Ronald Dworkin has suggested that utilitarian theory can be reconstituted in such a way as to make Mill's liberal thesis a consequence of it.[20] He distinguishes between personal and external preferences, and argues that all external preferences are not to be counted in the utilitarian justification for a political decision. A personal preference is a preference for a person's own enjoyment of some goods or opportunities, whereas an external preference is his preference for the assignment of goods or opportunities to others.[21] In other words, my personal preferences are about what I myself shall do or have, and my external preferences are about what other people should do or have. Dworkin argues that although individuals may in their personal lives act upon at least some of their external preferences, governments and legislators must base their decisions entirely on personal preferences. For example, the fact that the majority of personal preferences favour a sports stadium rather than an opera house counts as an argument for the stadium. But, on the other hand, the fact that the majority regard homosexuality as immoral does not count as an argument for legislating against homosexuality because the preferences here are external ones.[22] Similarly, although the fact that cruelty to children harms them is a relevant consideration, the different fact that the majority have an external preference which regards cruelty to children as wrong does not count. All external preferences, whether malevolent or altruistic, are to be excluded from the reconstituted utilitarian justification for political decisions.

Dworkin's argument raises two issues. The first is whether the consistency and internal coherence of utilitarianism dictates the exclusion of all external preferences. The second issue is whether, independently of its connection with utilitarianism, the exclusion of external preferences underlies Mill's defence of liberty. Dworkin takes sides on both these issues when he claims that Mill's arguments 'are not counter-utilitarian but, on the contrary, arguments in service of the only defensible form of utilitarianism' (p. 276).

But Dworkin does not succeed in showing that the exclusion of external preferences is demanded by a consistent application of utilitarianism itself rather than by the recognition of values independent of it. He points out that counting external preferences leads to the 'corruption' of utilitarianism.[23] Suppose that some people hold racist political theories that are contrary to the utilitarian's belief that each person is to count for one and no one for more than one. They believe that scarce medicine should be given to a white patient rather than to a black patient who needs it more. So the black man suffers because his assignment of goods and opportunities does not depend solely on the competition between the personal preferences of different people, but also on the fact that some whites think that he counts for less than a white man. Dworkin is certainly right that including external preferences will sometimes be self-defeating from the standpoint of personal preferences. But this does not show that utilitarianism is 'corrupted' unless it is already assumed that utilitarianism only counts personal preferences.

Dworkin also claims that counting external preferences is a form of double counting.[24] Suppose that many non-swimmers have external preferences for the pool rather than for the theatre because they approve of swimming and regard the theatre as immoral. If the non-swimmers' external preferences are counted, this will reinforce the personal preferences of swimmers, and the result is a form of double counting: 'each swimmer will have the benefit not only of his own preference, but also the preference of someone else who takes pleasure in his success.' (p. 235.) But there are two preferences here, and no single preference is counted twice.[25]

Dworkin argues that it is unfair to count external preferences because this will make the success of a person's personal preferences depend on the esteem and approval of others. Political decisions based on external preferences violate the fundamental right that people have to equal concern and respect. People should not suffer or be deprived of their liberty just because others think them less worthy of respect and concern.[26] But suppose that Dworkin is right here. This shows that discounting external preferences is demanded not by the internal requirements of utilitarianism as such, but rather by the requirement of fairness and the recognition of the fundamental right to equality of concern and respect. It has not been shown that utilitarianism is based on equality of concern and respect.

But Dworkin claims that utilitarianism owes its popularity to the assumption that it embodies this right to equal concern and respect. This is a different point which may or may not be true. If it is true, then the success of Dworkin's arguments will prove fatal to what he calls 'unrestricted utilitarianism' which counts external preferences. However it is at least arguable that one source of the popularity of utilitarianism lies in its neutrality between the different sources of people's happiness. Some people may find deeper and more abiding sources of happiness through their involvement with other people and through the promotion of various causes.[27] To exclude all external preferences in the utilitarian calculation is to cut off too much of what contributes to human happiness. In any case, is it always fair to exclude external preferences? Consider two variations on one of Dworkin's examples. First, suppose that many non-swimmers enjoy sitting around a swimming pool rather than being at the theatre. They are still expressing their personal preferences: they do not have to prefer a swimming pool to the theatre because they wish to swim. They enjoy the pool just as others enjoy the theatre even though they are not actors. But suppose now that many non-swimmers have personal preferences for the theatre, but they also have altruistic external preferences towards their children's enjoyment of swimming, and their external preferences for the pool is very much stronger than their personal preferences for the theatre. Dworkin would allow the swimming pool to be built on the basis of the personal preferences in the first example, but not on the basis of the external preferences in the second example. This seems unfair to the altruistic parents. They might be unable or unwilling to develop the personal preferences that would tip Dworkin's calculation in their favour.[28] They do not enjoy swimming, nor do they enjoy just sitting around a pool.

So in this case the exclusion of external preferences may be just as unfair as its inclusion in other contexts. This suggests that it is not the inclusion of external preferences as such that is unfair, but rather the content of the external preferences included. There is no reason why Mill's defence of liberty should commit him to the exclusion of all external preferences, nor is there any evidence to suggest that he would accept Dworkin's position.

VI. UTILITARIAN DEFENCE OF ABSOLUTE PROHIBITIONS

The difficulty of reconciling utilitarianism with Mill's absolute prohibition on interference with self-regarding conduct is that it seems obvious that there are cases where interference will maximize happiness. However an attempt has been made by Rolf E. Sartorius in his book *Individual Conduct and Social Norms* to show how a sophisticated utilitarian can support some absolute legal prohibitions.[29]

Sartorius's argument depends on there being a class of actions which satisfies the following conditions: (1) *most* acts belonging to that class are, on utilitarian grounds, wrong; (2) *some* acts belonging to that class are, on utilitarian grounds, right; and (3) most attempts to pick out the right acts from the wrong ones in that class fail because of the absence of any reliable criterion. A utilitarian will then have a case for absolutely prohibiting every act belonging to the class. He is aware that such an absolute prohibition will sometimes produce worse consequences, in utilitarian terms, than occasional successful interference. But since we do not know when such cases will arise, and the attempt to isolate them will produce undesirable consequences, the utilitarian aim of maximizing net satisfactions is best promoted by an absolute prohibition. An absolute prohibition of a certain class of acts means that if an act belongs to that class, then one is barred from making direct appeals to utility in deciding whether to perform it. Such direct appeals to utility will simply defeat the point of the absolute prohibition, which is to prevent mistakes being made in attempts to pick out the utilitarianly justified exceptions.

Sartorius thinks that Mill's case for individual liberty is based on an appeal to the type of argument presented above. Mill believed that absolute prohibition on legal intervention in self-regarding conduct satisfied the three conditions. However, Sartorius himself is of the opinion that, in the case of paternalistic intervention in self-regarding conduct, there are a few exceptions which can be reliably identified.

He gives as examples statutes making compulsory the wearing of protective helmets by motor-cyclists, and statutes prohibiting swimming after dark at unguarded beaches.[30] Of course utilitarians may disagree over purely factual details. In this case they may disagree about whether legal intervention in all types of self-regarding conduct satisfies the three conditions. They may also disagree about whether an absolute rule or a qualified one will best promote the utilitarian aim. However, in arriving at a decision, the facts to be taken into account by the utilitarian will include precisely what Mill was so eager to exclude, namely, the distress of those who are offended simply by the thought that others are privately engaged in acts which they regard as wrong, or which they merely dislike.[31] Sartorius does not think that giving due weight to such forms of distress will significantly affect the case for individual liberty. Here he may well be underestimating the strength and deep-seatedness of certain feelings and prejudices. But in any case whether or not he his right must surely depend on varying situations, and there is no reason to believe that 'in all nations with whom we need here concern ourselves', and at all times, the purely utilitarian case for liberty will be sufficiently powerful to protect all self-regarding conduct from intervention.

Mill himself was eager to provide a more secure basis for individual liberty. He did not wish its fate to depend on the strength and pervasiveness of the community's feelings towards self-regarding acts. When he argued that 'with the personal tastes and self-regarding concerns of individuals the public has no business to interfere',[32] the barrier he set up against invasions of freedom is much stronger than that which he would be entitled to if he had taken into account all the considerations that even a sophisticated utilitarian has to acknowledge. A utilitarian cannot disregard such considerations as the distress caused to the religious bigot and to others by self-regarding conduct, and the number of people who are so affected. All these will make a difference, and sometimes perhaps a decisive difference, to his calculation.

It is not Mill but his contemporary and vehement critic, James Fitzjames Stephen, who would agree with Sartorius in regarding as relevant the distress of outraged moral and religious sensibilities. But, unlike Sartorius, Stephen's utilitarian calculation led him to reject Mill's liberty principle. It is from the standpoint of a faithful and frightfully consistent utilitarian that Stephen wrote his sustained attack on Mill, *Liberty, Equality, Fraternity*.[33] Two remarks of his brother, Leslie Stephen, make this clear. In his biography of Fitzjames, Leslie Stephen wrote:

He holds that the doctrine of Mill's later books are really inconsistent with the doctrines of 'Logic' and 'Political Economy'. He is therefore virtually appealing from the new Utilitarians to the old. 'I am falling foul', he says in a letter, 'of John Mill in his modern and more humane mood — or rather, I should say, in his sentimental mood — which always makes me feel that he is a deserter from the proper principles of rigidity and ferocity in which he was brought up.'[34]

Elsewhere, Leslie Stephen again commented on *Liberty, Equality, Fraternity*: 'The most remarkable point is that the book is substantially a criticism of Mill's from the older utilitarian point of view. It shows, therefore, how Mill diverged from Bentham.'[35] It is worth spending some time on Fitzjames Stephen's view in order to illustrate the point that on purely utilitarian grounds the case for freedom in the self-regarding area may be much weaker than Sartorius supposes. Disagreements between utilitarians over allegedly factual matters will help to remind us how precarious a utilitarian defence of freedom can turn out to be, and how easy it is, in a world of uncertainty about the facts, to use the utilitarian calculation to arrive at almost any conclusion towards which one is already inclined.

As a follower of Bentham, Stephen attached value to the pleasures of malevolence. Bentham defined the pleasures of malevolence as 'the pleasures resulting from the view of any pain supposed to be suffered by the beings who become the objects of malevolence ... '[36] Even these pleasures are in themselves good because every pleasure is as such good, and as good as the same amount of any other pleasure. This being the case, there is no reason why legal and extra-legal sanctions should not in principle be applied to Mill's category of self-regarding conduct. In some communities it may well be that substantial pleasures of malevolence are aroused by the prospect of homosexuals being punished for their conduct.

These pleasures may in themselves still not be sufficient to outweigh the pain inflicted by the punishment of homosexuals, but they are always relevant, and are to be weighed on the same scale as the suffering caused by punishment. In some cases their addition to the scales may be enough to tip the utilitarian balance in favour of the legal prohibition of homosexuality where such prohibition is not backed by too severe penalties.

Stephen seemed to have some such argument in mind when he maintained, as against Mill, that 'there are acts of wickedness so gross and outrageous that, self-protection apart, they may be prevented as far as possible at any cost to the offender and punished, if they occur, with exemplary severity.'[37] Various arguments supporting this claim appear briefly. There is, for example, the Burkean argument that 'the fixed principles and institutions of society express not merely the present opinions of the ruling part of the community, but the accumulated results of centuries of experience.'[38] But his emphasis is on the desirability of hating criminals, and punishment is a way of gratifying this 'healthy natural sentiment' and of expressing society's moral condemnation of criminals.[39] Stephen's separation of these functions of punishment from the utilitarian function of preventing crime may give the impression that they have no utilitarian justification. But in fact Stephen himself referred to Bentham's view of the pleasures of malevolence in justifying the belief in the healthiness of gratifying the feelings of hatred and the desire for vengeance.[40] It is possible to reconstruct the retributive and denunciatory elements in Stephen's theory of punishment in purely Benthamite utilitarian terms. In a society where there is 'an overwhelming moral majority' who regard a particular type of self-regarding conduct as grossly immoral, a considerable amount of pleasures of malevolence will be derived from punishing those who engage in such acts. Stephen's insistence that it was the grosser forms of vice that he had in mind, and that there must be an overwhelming moral majority, may be taken to mean that for him unless these conditions are satisfied the utilitarian calculation would not favour the infliction of punishment.

The considerations invoked by Stephen against Mill help to

underline once again the fact that the strength of the utilitarian case for freedom will vary greatly with the different circumstances prevailing in different societies at different times. In so far as Mill intended his liberty principle to apply to all societies which have reached a certain stage of development, irrespective of all their other differences, it cannot be adequately defended solely on a utilitarian basis. Mill was able to commit himself so firmly and unreservedly to his principle only because he regarded as irrelevant some of the utilitarian considerations that both Stephen and Sartorius acknowledged, although with dramatically different results.

VII. TWO LEVELS OF MORAL THINKING

Another sophisticated version of utilitarianism, similar to Sartorius's, is to be found in R. M. Hare's idea of the two levels of moral thinking.[41] Hare himself does not discuss Mill's liberty principle, but a utilitarian, who is deeply committed to the principle, may well fall back on Hare's theory to explain and justify this commitment.

Level-1 in Hare's theory is the level of everyday practical moral thinking, whereas level-2 is the level of leisured moral thought when we have completely adequate knowledge of the facts. The utilitarian will of course adopt the utilitarian principle at level-2. But in everyday life a person, confronted with a moral problem, will often get the wrong answer if he applies the utilitarian principle directly because he lacks the time, or adequate information, or sufficient self-discipline. So at this level-1 it would be better to adopt other principles. The level-1 principles chosen will be those 'whose general acceptance leads to actions in accord with the best level-2 principles in most situations that are actually encountered'.[42] The level-1 principles will evolve with changing circumstances, and we use our level-2 principles to select the appropriate level-1 principles.

Now, it is arguable that Mill's liberty principle was put forward as a level-1 principle, and for that reason, even though it is based on utilitarianism at level-2, it need not always give the same answer as the direct application of the utilitarian principle. So far the argument is basically the same as that of Sartorius. But Hare is able to explain why violations of level-1 principles, even when know to be clearly justified on utilitarian grounds, will still be met with great repugnance by the utilitarian. On rare occasions we may have all the relevant information, and the normal, stressful conditions of everyday moral thinking may be absent. A utilitarian may then discover that his level-2 utilitarian principle dictates a course of action that violates a level-1 principle he has come to accept. Thus it may be clear, on a particular occasion, that breaking Mill's liberty principle will maximize net satisfactions. On this view a utilitarian should then act against the level-1 principle. But even so he will view the violation of the principle with great repugnance. This is because the level-1 principle has been inculcated in him as part of his self-education, and breaking it goes so much against the grain for him. In accepting the principle he has also acquired a set of motives and dispositions.

In this way one might be able to explain why Mill wished to exclude from his calculation the distress suffered by the religious bigot from the self-regarding conduct of others which violates his religious belief. At level-2 Mill, if he is a utilitarian, must take into account the distress. But, so the argument goes, he has in his self-education implanted in himself at level-1 a firm belief in the liberty principle which prohibits absolutely interference with self-regarding conduct. He is also trying to inculcate this principle in his fellow citizens. It is therefore understandable that he should be so attached to the principle, and should view its violation by others with great repugnance.

But there is one fatal flaw in this reconstruction of Mill's thinking. Mill was very much alive to the dangers of our beliefs hardening into prejudices and dogmas and, as we shall see in Chapter 8, he thought that freedom of discussion would help us avoid these dangers. He would therefore not wish to create a situation in which the level-1 principles are held in a rigid and inflexible manner. If he were a utilitarian, the way to ensure this would be to be constantly aware of the utilitarian underpinnings of all level-1 principles. So he could not allow the liberty principle to be too deeply ingrained in himself and in others. He could not develop in himself and in others too strong a disposition to disregard those utilitarian considerations which are inconsistent with the recognition of the liberty principle. If the liberty principle is simply a level-1 principle, which has to be revised in the light of changing circumstances by an appeal to utilitarianism at level-2, then it is difficult to see how Mill could have argued so forcefully and unqualifiedly for the exclusion of some utilitarianly relevant considerations. So once again Mill's attachment to the liberty principle seems deeper and stronger than it would be if it were a level-1 principle.

The arguments of Sartorius and Hare, while consistent with a sophisticated utilitarianism, differ from those more commonly used by utilitarians. A more usual approach adopted by utilitarians is to treat subordinate moral principles as mere 'rules of thumb' whose application will generally, though not invariably, serve the utilitarian end of maximizing happiness or net satisfactions. Such 'rules of thumb' are often necessary if people are to have reasonably clear guidance as to how they are to act in particular situations. As we have already noted earlier, it is, for example, much easier to know what is required if one is asked to tell the truth than if one is asked to maximize happiness. Now, it has been suggested that the various liberal principles to be extracted from Mill's essay are not, in spite of what Mill says, absolute, but rather 'rules of thumb' which may be breached when breaking them will better serve the utilitarian end.[43] For example, there is to be a presumption against state or social intervention to prevent individuals from harming themselves, and there is also a very strong presumption against interfering with a person's conduct on the ground that it violates the shared morality of society. However these presumptions are rebuttable on utilitarian grounds.

This interpretation of Mill is based on the assumption that he is clearly a utilitarian, and that therefore any account of his case for liberty must be consistent with utilitarianism. But this is precisely the assumption that I have challenged in this chapter. By excluding some pleasures and pains, and some satisfactions, as irrelevant, Mill altered the content of the notion of utility or happiness. To show that he is still a utilitarian, it is therefore necessary not merely to fit his arguments for liberty into the formal structure of a particular model of moral reasoning adopted by utilitarians, but also to establish that the substantive considerations he appealed to, or ruled out, are consistent with some version of utilitariansim. This has so far not been done.

VIII. REASONS FOR INTERVENTION

Mill's claim that individual libertry in the area of self-regarding actions should be absolute has given rise to much misunderstanding of his position. His critics have argued that there is no area of conduct with which the state is not sometimes justified in interfering. Thus Lord Devlin seems to think that Mill's liberalism commits him to invoking 'a principle that exempts all private immorality always from the operation of the law'.[44] Against this Devlin maintains that there can be no 'theoretical limits' to the power of the state to legislate against what is considered immoral conduct. It may be argued that if a man gets drunk every night in the privacy of his home, this should not concern anyone else. But, Devlin asks, what sort of a society would it be if half the population got drunk every night?[45] His point here seems to be that when certain types of private immoralities increase they may have very harmful effects even though they may be quite harmless when they are confined to a few people.

Devlin has obviously misunderstood Mill. It is not essential to Mill's position that there should be an area of conduct which must always remain completely free from intervention. The absoluteness of Mill's barrier against intervention, or the 'theoretical limit' he sets to the power of the state and society to exercise coercion, is of a different kind. There are certain reasons for intervention in the conduct of individuals which must always be ruled out as irrelevant. Even when intervention is justified in a particular case it is on the basis of certain reasons rather than others: 'No person ought to be punished for being drunk, but a soldier or a policeman should be punished for being drunk on duty.' (p. 138.)

Let us suppose that there are no actions which only affect others because they are disliked, or regarded as immoral or offensive. All actions also affect non-consenting persons in other ways. Mill's case for freedom is still not undermined. There are various reasons why people may wish to interfere with the conduct of others. Mill's point is that the case for intervention must rest on reasons other than, for example, the mere dislike or disapproval of the conduct. If these other reasons are insufficient, no additional weight is given by citing the dislike and disapproval.[46] Consider, for example, the case of pornography. Mill's liberty principle rules out the argument that the sale of pornography should be prohibited simply because the majority regard the sale and reading of pornography as immoral. But this does not settle the issue of whether pornography should be prohibited, because other reasons have been given for the prohibition. Thus it is often claimed that reading pornography is a cause of crime, especially sexual crime. If this is true, it would be accepted by Mill as a reason for prohibition. But the matter is to be settled in the light of the available evidence. It is just because such evidence does not seem to support the factual claims made that people are tempted to fall back on their repugnance towards pornography. The acceptance of Mill's principle will prevent them from doing that, and instead confine the debate to an assessment of the evidence for the allegedly harmful, or beneficial, effects of reading pornography.

What is crucial to Mill's defence of liberty is therefore his belief that certain reasons for intervention — paternalistic, moralistic, and gut reactions — are irrelevant, whereas the prevention of harm to others is always relevant.

3

Morality and Utility

I. MORAL AND NON-MORAL APPRAISALS OF CONDUCT

In arguing that Mill's liberty principle is inconsistent with utilitarianism, I have assumed that utilitarianism is a moral doctrine about the rightness or wrongness of actions. But some recent interpretations of Mill have argued that, although he subscribed to a principle of utility, his version of it is not that of a moral principle but rather a more general principle on the basis of which all appraisals of conduct, whether moral or non-moral, are made. Moral appraisals of conduct are merely one type of evaluations derivable from the principle of utility, and Mill has a more restricted theory of morality than is commonly assumed. How does this account of Mill's principle of utility and his theory of morality affect the nature of his case for liberty? The pioneering work of Alan Ryan in this area has illuminated previously neglected aspects of his thought.[1] Ryan's thesis is that the distinction between self- and other-regarding conduct 'is at the heart of the distinction between moral and non-moral appraisal of actions'.[2] Self-regarding conduct belongs to the areas of prudence and aesthetics and not those of morality and law which are concerned with other-regarding conduct. It is only in the other-regarding sphere that sanctions or punishment may be applied. In deciding whether to use legal sanctions or the sanction of public opinion and social disapproval to deter wrongful acts, we take account of the relative social costs involved. Moral judgements are based on the harm the agent knowingly does to others. But self-regarding conduct, which does not harm others, lies outside this moral realm. Such conduct may not therefore be punished, or subjected to compulsion, although it is a 'fit matter for entreaty, expostulation, exhortation'.[3]

Ryan's work has led to important developments in the interpretation of Mill.[4] It is necessary to examine in greater detail the distinction between the moral and the non-moral

42

spheres of conduct to see whether it provides a new basis for
Mill's defence of individual liberty. I shall begin by outlining
Mill's theory of 'the Art of Life' as propounded in *A System
of Logic*, Book VI, Chapter xii. This will help in the understanding of his division between the moral and the non-moral
spheres.

II. THE ART OF LIFE

Mill distinguishes between science and art, and he regards
morality as an art. Science is concerned with matters of fact,
whereas art is concerned with rules and precepts which enjoin
or recommend that something should be the case. The propo-
sitions of art are about what *ought* to be or *should be* the
case; those of science are expressed in the indicative mood
and are about what *is* or *will be*. Every particular art has an
end or purpose:

> The builder's art assumes that it is desirable to have buildings; architec-
> ture (as one of the fine arts), that it is desirable to have them beautiful
> or imposing. The hygienic and medical arts assume, the one that preserva-
> tion of health, the other that the cure of disease, are fitting and desirable
> ends.[5]

Once a particular art has proposed a certain end as desirable,
science investigates the means by which this end can be
attained. The performance of those actions constituting the
means is then pronounced by art as desirable, and rules or
precepts are generated. Thus the relation between art and
science can be characterized in the form of a deductive model
with the major premiss supplied by art and the minor premiss
by science. From these a conclusion in the form of a rule or
precept is drawn. Mill's thesis can be roughly represented as
follows:[6]

Major Premiss: *E* is desirable   (where *E* is defined
by a particular art).

Minor Premiss: Actions of type
a will bring about
E   (theorem of science).

Conclusion: Therefore *a* is desirable.

Mill points out that the rules or precepts for guiding conduct

are to be considered provisional: 'But they do not all super-
sede the propensity of going through (when circumstances
permit) the scientific process requisite for framing a rule
from the data of the particular case before us.'[7] In a particular case, because of unusual circumstances, following a
rule may not attain the desirable end. Again, in certain
situations, following a rule will lead to a conflict with some
other end which is more desirable.

The possibility of conflict between the ends of various arts
points to the need for determining the relative importance of
these ends, or the order of precedence between them. This is
the province for that body of doctrine which Mill calls
variously the Art of Life, Teleology, the Doctrine of Ends,
and the Principles of Practical Reason. The function of the
Art of Life is to justify the ends of subordinate arts, and to
establish an order of priority among them. The Art of Life
has three departments: 'Morality, Prudence or Policy, and
Aesthetics, the Right, the Expedient, and the Beautiful or
Noble, in human conduct and works'.[8] Elsewhere, in *Utilitarianism*, Mill distinguishes morality from 'the remaining
provinces of Expediency and Worthiness'.[9] And in the essay
on Bentham he refers to the various aspects possessed by
actions: 'a *moral* aspect, that of its *right* and *wrong*; its
aesthetic aspect, or that of its beauty; its *sympathetic* aspect
or that of its *loveableness'*.[10] But what is clear is that moral
appraisals are not the only appraisals of conduct. There are
also prudential and aesthetic appraisals.

The next step Mill takes is to argue that there must be only
one ultimate principle or standard for assessing the value of
various ends and their order of precedence. If there were
more than one ultimate principle, then the same action
might be derived from one principle while running foul of
another. It would then be necessary to appeal to yet another
principle to settle conflicts between these two principles. So
the Art of Life has only one ultimate principle, and this
principle is common to all the departments of the Art. Mill
then asserts that

the general principle to which all rules of practice ought to conform,
and the test by which they should be tried, is that of conduciveness
to the happiness of mankind or rather of all sentient beings; in other

words, that the promotion of happiness is the ultimate principle of Teleology.[11]

In a *A System of Logic* he does not attempt to justify this claim, but he inserts a footnote which draws attention to his famous 'proof' of utility in *Utilitarianism*. So for Mill the principle of utility is the ultimate principle of the whole Art of Life, and is therefore the ultimate basis for moral as well as non-moral appraisals of conduct.

Mill's account of the Art of Life raises several problems. D. G. Brown has drawn attention to the serious difficulty of stating the principle of utility in such a way as to enable it to perform the important role Mill has cast for it. Brown himself favours the formulation, 'Happiness is the only thing desirable as an end.'[12] Another problem is how exactly the different departments of the Art of Life are to be demarcated from one another. Mill says much more about the province of morality than he does about the other areas, and I shall focus on one detailed interpretation of his theory of morality which takes account of these divisions within the Art of Life. My purpose is to ascertain whether, assuming the correctness of this theory of morality, we have here a new weapon within the utilitarian armoury for defending the individual's liberty to engage in self-regarding actions.

III. LYONS ON MILL'S THEORY OF MORALITY

David Lyons has recently developed a complex, though apparently still incomplete, interpretation of Mill's theory of morality.[13] Lyons places great weight on a passage in *Utilitarianism* which in part reads:

We do not call anything wrong, unless we mean to imply that a person ought to be punished in some way or other for doing it; if not by law, by the opinion of his fellow-creatures; if not by opinion, by the reproaches of his own conscience. This seems the real turning point of the distinction between morality and simple expediency. It is part of the notion of Duty in every one of its forms, that a person may rightfully be compelled to fulfil it. Duty is a thing which may be *exacted* from a person, as one exacts a debt. . . . Reasons of prudence, or the interest of other people, may militate against actually exacting it; but the person himself, it is clearly understood, would not be entitled to complain. There are other things, on the contrary, which we wish that people should do, which we like or admire them for doing, perhaps dislike or despise them for not doing, but yet admit that they are not bound to do; it is not a case of moral obligation; we do not blame them, that is, we do not think that they are proper objects for punishment.[14] Here Mill is linking the notion of morality with 'punishment' or sanctions. Morality is concerned with right and wrong, with duty and obligation, and when we call an action wrong we imply that 'punishment' of it, or some sort of sanction against it, would be justified. But sanctions are of different types. Legal penalties and social disapprobation are external sanctions, whereas guilt feelings, or the reproaches of one's conscience, are internal sanctions. Lyons observes that Mill's point here is a conceptual one about the concept of moral wrongness, and is independent of his subscription to utilitarianism. But utilitarianism is invoked in determining when sanctions are justifiably applied, and the type of sanctions to be applied.

According to Lyons, Mill regards the internal sanction as basic.[15] Hence an act is wrong when guilt feelings for it would be warranted. The application of external sanctions to wrong acts will not always be appropriate as there are additional disutilities involved. But when the stakes are high, then the use of external sanctions can be justified on utilitarian grounds. The external sanctions applied to wrong acts operate not only after the acts have been done, but also before the acts in the form of threats to discourage the acts from being committed. To discourage wrong acts, sanctions will be attached to coercive rules which serve to direct conduct. The external sanctions are attached to legal rules and to informal social rules which embody the conventional morality of the society. In the case of internal sanctions, the link is not directly with social rules but with a person's conscience. The personal values, violation of which produces guilt feelings, can be conceived of as guides to conduct. But the more important way in which personal values produce directives for conduct is through their connection with the community's moral code. The common morality is constituted by the shared personal values of its members. So the internal sanctions will, to some extent at least, be attached to the same set of rules as the external sanctions of social disapproval. Both the existence of informal social rules and their effectiveness in directing conduct depend on the widespread internalization within the community of the relevant values.[16]

Since even the internal sanctions are linked, in the way described, to social rules, it follows that if we are to show that an act is wrong, we have to show that a coercive social rule against it is justified. The justification of a coercive social rule establishes a moral obligation to act in accordance with it. In the absence of another overriding obligation, it is wrong to breach the rule.

The justification for the coercive rule must always be on utilitarian grounds. But Mill's position, on Lyon's interpretation, is unlike that of the act utilitarian who justifies particular acts by their utility. According to the act utilitarian, an act is wrong if, compared to all alternative acts, it does not maximize utility. In Mill's theory of morality, on the other hand, it is not just the utility of the act which has to be taken into account. One has also to determine the utility of regulating actions of that type by means of a coercive social rule. There are therefore acts which the act utilitarian would regard as wrong, but which Mill will not.

It is also clear that there are acts which one has a moral obligation to perform even though they do not maximize utility. This is because Lyons's account of Mill's theory of morality makes it into a version of rule utilitarianism. But it differs from ordinary versions of rule utilitarianism in that the latter subjects only rules, and never acts directly, to the utilitarian test. In ordinary versions of rule utilitarianism, an act is right if it falls under a rule that, if generally adopted or followed, will produce maximum utility, as compared with alternative rules. But, according to Lyons, it is only Mill's theory of morality which conforms to this rule utilitarian structure. Non-moral evaluations of conduct are made, not via their conformity to maximally useful rules, but by a direct appeal to the principle of utility.

On Lyons's interpretation, Mill's principle of utility does not lay down a moral requirement or obligation always to maximize utility. Like Brown, Lyons believes that the principle of utility refers to an end, happiness, in terms of which all conduct must be evaluated. Mill would prefer one act to another if it promoted greater utility or happiness. An act is regarded as 'inexpedient' when it fails to maximize utility.

But an inexpedient act is not necessarily a wrong act. When the principle of utility is applied directly to acts, it does not yield a moral judgement about the acts, but rather evaluations of their expediency.

As we have noted, Lyons's account allows for the possibility of a conflict between a requirement of morality and the end of maximizing happiness. Lyons himself raises this problem but he expresses uncertainty about how Mill would solve it. He is unsure whether Mill's commitment to the end of happiness necessarily implies the subordination of all other values.[17] But it looks as if, even on Lyons's own interpretation of Mill's principle of utility, this uncertainty is misplaced. For Lyons maintains: 'Mill is committed fundamentally to the end of happiness, and thereby to *whatever* means best serve that end.'[18] The end is that of maximizing happiness. Suppose now that the best means of serving the end of maximizing happiness is to perform a morally wrong act. Surely Mill is committed to sacrificing morality in the interests of serving this end. Mill's principle of utility is the sole ultimate principle of the Art of Life, and it must therefore be the final court of appeal in all conflicts between other principles belonging to the various departments of the Art of Life. If the principle of utility requires the maximization of happiness, then morality must give way if it hinders this ultimate end. Morality is only one generally effective means of promoting the end of maximizing happiness.

There is nothing in Mill's analysis of the concept of morality to show that the requirements of morality must take precedence over all non-moral considerations. In any case, the question of what one should ultimately do has to be settled in the light of one's substantive values. A conceptual analysis of the notion of moral obligation can determine only the terms in which we state what we should do; it cannot settle for us the choice between alternative courses of action. Thus we may not have a moral obligation always to maximize happiness, but from this alone it does not follow that we should not always act to maximize happiness, even when this involves the violation of our moral obligations.

IV. SELF-REGARDING CONDUCT AND THE NON-MORAL SPHERE

The upshot of the foregoing discussion is that even if self-regarding conduct belongs to the non-moral sphere, this is not a reason why it should always be exempted from intervention. If intervention maximizes happiness, then the utilitarian is committed to it, whether or not it can be said to be morally required, or even to be morally wrong. This crucial point cannot be avoided even if we modify Mill's theory of morality so that there will be no conflict between moral and non-moral values. No matter how one carves out the territory between morality and the rest of the Art of Life, there can be no secure refuge from intervention for self-regarding conduct so long as Mill's principle of utility is regarded as seeking the end of maximizing happiness, and happiness is interpreted along classical or preference utilitarian lines. I shall briefly illustrate this.

Suppose that morally obligatory acts are a sub-class of acts which maximize happiness. We may then add that 'self-regarding faults' consist of failures to maximize happiness outside the morally required area. But this will not help unless the application of sanctions is restricted to failures to perform morally required acts. But why should the utilitarian accept that? If the ultimate end is to maximize happiness, then sanctions should be applied *whenever* it will maximize happiness to apply them, irrespective of the type of acts to which they are applied. So either we restrict the scope of morality, in which case some sanctions may be applied to non-moral acts; or else we allow morality to have the monopoly of the use of sanctions, in which case we have to extend morally required conduct to all cases where the application of sanctions will maximize happiness.

If we adopt the latter position, then we get the following theory of morality. Acts are morally wrong when it will maximize happiness to apply sanctions to them. So some acts which fail to maximize happiness are again not morally wrong. It also does not follow from this theory that *only* acts which fail to maximize happiness are morally wrong, for on perhaps rare occasions it may maximize happiness to apply sanctions to acts which themselves maximize utility. But what is the difference between this revised utilitarian theory and ordinary act utilitarianism? We have here a distinction without a practical difference.

We saw in the previous chapter that the act utilitarian distinguishes between the morality of an act and the morality of praising, or blaming, or punishing someone for the performance of the act. For example, because of the additional costs of inflicting punishment, happiness may not be maximized in a particular case by punishing someone for a wrong act. So the act utilitarian is not committed to applying sanctions to all acts that he regards as morally wrong. He will apply sanctions only when it maximizes utility to do so, and in this the practical implication of his view is exactly the same as that of revised utilitarianism. Some acts which act utilitarianism regards as wrong, the revised utilitarianism does not, but for the act utilitarian the application of sanctions is a further question. Revised utilitarianism, on the other hand, by regarding as morally wrong only acts to which the application of sanctions will maximize happiness, settles the issue of applying sanctions when it determines the act to be wrong. There is for a supporter of revised utilitarianism no further question to be raised. But on both views, sanctions are only applicable when happiness is maximized. Both doctrines will apply sanctions to exactly the same acts, and refrain from doing so on exactly the same occasions. So on both views, if applying sanctions to self-regarding conduct will maximize happiness, then it should be done. However, if it is assumed that it will never maximize happiness to interfere with self-regarding conduct, then on the revised utilitarian view, such conduct will never be wrong. In that case the act utilitarian will also support non-intervention, whether or not on his own view self-regarding conduct is morally wrong. But we have come a full circle and have to face all the same problems discussed in the previous chapter of showing that the assumption is well based. What we need, and do not have, is an argument to demonstrate that it will never maximize happiness to interfere with, or to apply sanctions to, self-regarding actions.

I conclude therefore that the various reinterpretations of Mill's moral theory do not alter the problem of reconciling his defence of self-regarding conduct with utilitarianism. We have so far been discussing issues raised by Mill's account of self-regarding conduct. We should now turn our attention to the other side of his distinction. Other-regarding actions may be interfered with as they harm others. But what does Mill mean by 'harm', and what is the scope and basis of his claim that the prevention of harm to others may justify intervention in the conduct of individuals?

4

Harm to Others

Mill's liberty principle allows intervention in the freedom of the individual in order to prevent harm to others. Although the infliction of bodily injury is one type of harm, Mill obviously did not regard it as synonymous with the whole range of harmful conduct. For example, he regarded theft and unwarranted invasions of liberty as also harmful. But once the notion of harm is extended beyond that of bodily injury, the problem is to find somewhere to stop without arbitrariness or without invoking highly disputable values. It is sometimes said that the notion of harm is so deeply value-impregnated that there can be no general agreement among people with different values about what is harmful.[1]

I. HARM AS THE NON-FULFILMENT OF DESIRE

Within the utilitarian tradition, the wide notion of harm as the frustration or non-fulfilment of any desire whatever recommends itself. Perhaps the clearest account of this idea of harm is that developed by R. M. Hare who maintains that 'To harm somebody is to act against his interests.'[2] The notion of interests is conceptually linked to that of desires, or that of wanting. So to say that an act would harm somebody is to say that 'it would, or might in possible circumstances prevent some desire of his from being realized.'[3] Hare uses the notions of desiring or wanting in a wide sense such that a person desires something if and only if, other things being equal, he will seek to do, or to get, or to retain it. Thus for Hare, to harm someone is to frustrate the fulfilment of his desires.[4] Hare in fact adopts preference utilitarianism rather than classical utilitarianism. The preference utilitarian seeks to maximize the net satisfaction of desires. The classical utilitarian, on the other hand, is concerned with maximizing pleasant experiences or states of mind. He will therefore confine the notion of harm to the frustration of a desire, where the frustration in question is a *felt* experience. The fulfilment or non-fulfilment of desires which merely involves the coming into existence of a state of affairs, but which does not produce pleasant or unpleasant experiences, will not be relevant. So, unlike Hare, the classical utilitarian will not think that a person has been harmed if the person is unaware, and will never be aware, that a desire of his is unfulfilled. And the dead too cannot therefore be harmed since they are incapable of having any experiences.[5]

However, there will be agreement between the classical utilitarian and the preference utilitarian over a very wide range of harmful conduct. For example, if a religious person is offended by the conduct of others even in private, or if his desire that they should change their behaviour is not complied with, then he is, on both views, harmed. Again, if a fanatical Nazi desires that all Jews be put to the gas chamber, and his desire is not realized, then he has been harmed. Of course sending Jews to the gas chamber will also harm them, and to a greater degree than the harm inflicted on the Nazi if his desire is not fulfilled. But Hare himself points out that

If, per impossible, there were any such real fanatic, i.e. a fanatic whose desire to be rid of Jews really did outweigh in strength the desires of all the Jews not to be rid of, then, both on the utilitarian view and on mine, the desire ought to be complied with.[6]

It is an implication of Hare's position that an innocent Jew, going about his daily concerns without bothering anybody, would none the less be harming fanatical Nazis simply because their desires that he be put in a gas chamber are not complied with. Indeed the more fanatical the Nazis, the greater are their desires to eliminate the Jew, and hence the stronger is the utilitarian case for sending the Jew to the gas chamber. Hare himself believes that in real life, situations of this kind, where the number of fanatical Nazis far exceeds the number of Jews such that satisfactions will be maximized if Jews are exterminated, will not occur. This optimism may be well placed. But it is difficult to have the same confidence with regard to less extreme cases of racial and religious intolerance and prejudice towards minority groups, in which what is demanded by the majority is inferior treatment of minorities, or the withholding of some rights, or perhaps their deportation. In some real-life situations, the results of a truly neutral utilitarian calculation may be very indecisive as between liberal and illiberal solutions, with everything depending on the intensity of feelings and the way the numbers swing. No one, who is concerned with the freedom of minorities in the face of a hostile and prejudiced majority, can be happy with this situation. The fact that many utilitarians are convinced that the calculation will easily support a policy of toleration is a tribute to their latent liberalism rather than to their professed utilitarianism, or their understanding of the depth and intractability of racial and religious prejudices.

It is evident that Mill does not accept this wide, utilitarianly based notion of harm. He says explicitly that we should be free to do what we like without interference from others 'so long as what we do does not harm them, even though they should think our conduct foolish, perverse, or wrong'.[7] Here he is contrasting two different types of adverse effects on others. If our conduct affects others simply because they regard it as 'foolish, perverse, or wrong', then we do not *harm* them, whatever else we may be said to have inflicted on them. So Mill cannot believe that the non-fulfilment of their desires that we stop our 'foolish, perverse, or wrong' conduct is a form of harm to them. Here it is important to distinguish between two different positions. The first is that conduct which adversely affects others in these ways harms them, but the harm is slight and is always outweighed by the good of non-intervention. This is not Mill's position. If it were, then he would have to regard such conduct as other-regarding, which he plainly does not. His position is that the conduct does not harm others at all, and therefore no question of balancing harm against harm, or harm against good, arises. The former position is compatible with utilitarianism, but Mill's position is not.

However, it may be argued that a consistent utilitarian is not forced to accept the wide notion of harm that Mill so clearly rejects. He can, for example, regard as harmful conduct which causes a net balance of pain over pleasure. In that case it is not necessary for him to consider all actions which cause pain or distress as harmful. For example, homosexual conduct between consenting adults in private may distress others, but if it invariably produces more pleasure than pain, then it is not, on this view, harmful. This is a notion of harm that the utilitarian can accept because it takes into account all forms of pain or distress in determining whether an act is harmful. But it is evident that Mill does not accept this notion of harm either. Mill believes that the relevant calculation comes into play only *after* it has been shown that an action is harmful, whereas on this account the utilitarian calculation determines whether that action is harmful. Thus Mill writes:

As soon as any part of a person's conduct affects prejudicially the interest of others, society has jurisdiction over it, and the question whether the general welfare will or will not be promoted by interfering with it, becomes open to discussion. But there is no room for entertaining any such question when a person's conduct affects the interests of no persons besides himself, or needs not affect them unless they like (all the persons concerned being of full age, and the ordinary amount of understanding.)[8]

II. MILL'S CONCEPT OF HARM

Mill's concept of harm has to be pieced together from some of his general remarks, and from the examples he gives of conduct harmful to others. Apart from the infliction of bodily injury, the sorts of harmful conduct that Mill has in mind seem to involve the infringement of certain rules. Thus he writes about the person who has 'infringed the rules necessary for the protection of his fellow-creatures, individually or collectively'.[9] The rules in question do not just protect individuals directly, but also via the protection of society. In *Utilitarianism* Mill says that 'a human being is capable of apprehending a community of interest between himself and the human society of which he forms a part, such that any conduct which threatens the security of the society generally, is threatening to his own.' (p. 48.) There too he traces the 'sentiment of justice' to the idea of a harm to society: 'just persons resenting a hurt to society, though not otherwise a hurt to themselves, and not resenting a hurt to themselves, however painful unless it be of the kind which society has a common interest with them in the repression of' (p. 48). In *On Liberty* he regards many of our duties to others, which are enforceable by law or social disapprobation, as arising out of our having received the protection of society.

Though society is not founded on a contract, and though no good purpose is answered by inventing a contract in order to deduce social obligations from it, every one who receives the protection of society owes a return for the benefit, and the fact of living in society renders it indispensable that each should be bound to observe a certain line of conduct towards the rest. (p. 132.)

It is in the context of an ongoing, viable society that individuals enjoy the benefits that Mill mentions, and a central part of Mill's concept of harm is tied to the infringement of those rules which are necessary for the continued survival of society. The nature of these rules can be illuminated with the help of Hart's discussion in *The Concept of Law* of what he calls 'the minimum content of natural law'.[10] Hart argues that, given only certain very obvious generalizations or truisms about human nature and the world in which we live, 'there are certain rules which any social organisation must contain if it is to be viable.'[11]

First, human beings are vulnerable to attack by their fellow men, and unless therefore there are rules prohibiting the use of violence in killing and in inflicting bodily harm, it would be pointless for men to have any other rules governing their conduct. So given that men wish to survive, any society must have rules regulating conduct in these areas. Although men's physical and intellectual capacities vary, they do not differ so greatly that one person, on his own, can permanently dominate over the others. The fact of approximate equality between men, and the further fact that men's altruism is limited and they are sometimes tempted to inflict injuries on one another, means that social life would be intolerable if there were no rules restraining men's aggression. Again, men need resources like food, and these are limited. In order that food may be securely grown, there must be rules forbidding unauthorized interference and theft. So some minimal rules respecting property are necessary. And, as society gets bigger and more complex, the adequate cultivation of resources calls for division of labour, and this in turn introduces new rules. In order that men may transfer, exchange, and sell their products, certain rules acknowledging the binding nature of promises and contracts are needed. These give men confidence that others will keep their promises and contracts, and thereby make co-operation possible and mutually beneficial. So in these ways we see the necessity of rules protecting the physical integrity of the person, respecting property, and rules recognizing the binding nature of promises and contracts. But since some men are not able to resist the temptation to break these rules in order to promote their immediate interests, it is also necessary to have institutions which enforce the rules and compel obedience by detecting and punishing malefactors.

A universal concept of harm, common to all societies, can be based on Hart's account of the importance of these types of rules. We can say that harmful conduct consists in the infringement of those rules, and the impairment of those institutions, necessary to the viability of society. Something like this is what Mill seems to have in mind, and most of his examples of harm to others can be captured within this notion of harm. But there are at least three complications which must be added, the first two being relatively minor while the third is major.

First, then, we have so far been concerned with those rules which are needed for the survival of any society. But it may be that over and above these rules, there are also other rules which are necessary to the survival of a particular society.[12] In his discussion in the essay on Coleridge of the conditions of social stability,[13] Mill shows his awareness of this possibility. If the concept of harm is tied to the viability of society, then of course Mill would accept that infringements of rules without which a particular society will not survive is harmful in much the same way as infringements of the universal rules. The real problem here is to show that in a given case a certain set of rules is really needed if a particular society is to survive at all, and not just to survive unchanged in its present form.

The second complication relates to the infringement of liberty. That Mill regards at least certain interferences with individual liberty as harmful is shown in the following two quotations from *Utilitarianism*.

The moral rules which forbid mankind to hurt one another (in which one must never forget to include wrongful interference with each other's freedom) are more vital to human well-being than any maxims, however important, which only point out the best mode of managing some department of human affairs. (p. 55.)

The next quotation is also taken from his discussion of justice, and in fact appears only a few lines later:

Thus the moralities which prevent every individual from being harmed by others, either directly or by being hindered in his freedom of pursuing his own good, are at once those which he himself has most at heart, and those which he has the strongest interest in publishing and enforcing by word and deed. (p. 56.)

The idea that 'wrongful interference with each other's freedom' is harmful, though not 'directly', can be elaborated in the following manner. The violations of certain rules are directly harmful. But a corollary of this is that conduct which does not involve the breach of these rules is not harmful. Mill then regards interference with non-harmful conduct as indirectly harmful. The type of wrongful interference with others' freedom that Mill has in mind relates to interference with the freedom of people to lead their own lives within the coercive framework of the central rules of the society. There is no doubt about the importance Mill attaches to such freedom.

But sometimes it looks as if Mill wishes to treat a much wider area of interference with freedom as harmful. He writes, 'all restraint, *qua* restraint, is an evil',[14] and this is in the context of his discussion of the doctrine of Free Trade. Trade, he says, is 'a social act', and so restrictions on trade do not violate his liberty principle: they fall within the legitimate scope of social intervention. Yet it counts as an argument against restricting free trade, though not as a conclusive argument, that freedom is restricted. The force of saying that trade is a social act is that people can be harmed by trading activities. So it follows that interference with some harmful conduct is itself also harmful. But how far is Mill prepared to go? If a group of religious fanatics prevent others from practising their different religion, the fanatics harm others by interfering with their non-harmful conduct. But now if the state coercively stops the actions of the fanatics, this is interference with their harmful conduct. Is this latter interference also harmful, as at first it might appear to be, because 'all restraint, *qua* restraint, is an evil'? Mill believes that fanatics are never justified in interfering with the non-harmful conduct of others simply because they disapprove of it. In the context of his defence of individual freedom, this implies that the state is justified in stopping the unwarranted actions of fanatics. But if now the rightness of state intervention is a matter of balancing consequences, with the harm of the inter- vention itself to be thrown into the scale, then this additional harm might just tip the scale against intervention. So it would appear that Mill cannot regard all intervention with harmful conduct as themselves harmful. There is some indication of this line of thought when he writes:

To be held to rigid rules of justice for the sake of others, develops the feelings and capacities which have the good of others for their objects. But to be restrained in things not affecting their good, by their mere displeasure, develops nothing valuable, except such force of character as may unfold itself in resisting the restraint.[15]

It would therefore appear that for Mill interference with liberty is harmful only if it restricts non-harmful conduct, or if it restricts conduct in areas covered by the necessary rules, which I shall call the 'social domain'. This whole idea of a social domain leads to the third, and major, complication in Mill's concept of harm.

I have said that central to Mill's notion of harm is the idea of infringing the rules necessary to the viability of society. But this is oversimplified because it is not necessary to have specific rules, but only to have rules regulating certain areas of conduct, namely the social domain. Any one of many different sets of rules in the social domain will be enough to ensure the viability of society. For example, a society needs some property rules, but it does not need any particular set of property rules. It can survive whether the rules allow for private ownership of the means of production or only public ownership. It can survive even if some groups in society are unfairly discriminated against and are not permitted to acquire certain resources.[16] If harm consists in the infringement of the specific rules in a society, then what is harmful will vary from society to society. The notion of harm will be too closely linked to the particular values of different societies to serve Mill's purpose.

To avoid this high degree of relativity, Mill seems to fall back on something like the following argument. Since, in any society, it is necessary to have a common set of rules in the social domain, the infringement of the existing rules must be regarded as harmful. But, on the other hand, it is always possible to conceive of alternative sets of rules in the social domain which, if they replace the existing set, will also ensure the survival of society, and may in addition be more desirable from other points of view. Alternative sets of rules therefore compete with one another, and anyone who is adversely affected by the operation of existing rules can claim to be harmed by them, since they are not the only rules available. Mill's account of justice in *Utilitarianism* gives some support to this reading of him. We have already seen that for him unjust acts are harmful. He also says that 'it is just to respect, unjust to violate, the *legal rights* of any one.' (p. 40.) This means, for example, that it is unjust and therefore harmful to violate a person's property rights. But Mill goes on to say that some laws are bad, and confer rights which *ought* not to exist. A bad law causes harm by infringing the *moral* rights of persons.

The recognition that the operation of existing rules in the social domain can cause harm introduces a new element into Mill's concept of harm. Given that alternative sets of rules in the social domain are consistent with the viability of society, the question arises: Which particular set of rules should be adopted? Mill's answer here is utilitarian: the ideal rules are those which best conform to the utilitarian standard. The choice of the ideal rules will have to take into account the fact that rules in different parts of the social domain interact. There is a particularly close link between the property rules and the rules regulating the keeping of contracts. The distribution of income and resources in a community affects the bargaining powers of the parties to contracts, and therefore influences the types of contracts that are likely to be made. But the enforcement of contracts with certain contents in turn also affects the distribution of the resources of a community. So the ideal rules will have something to say not just about the distribution of income and resources, but also about the enforceability of certain types of contracts which affects this distribution.

An important implication of all this is that there is no necessary connection between Millian liberalism and either a doctrine of economic *laissez-faire*, or a theory of the minimal functions of the state. It is possible to combine Mill's liberty principle with, for example, a belief in socialism. The way in which the resources of a community are distributed falls within the social domain, and therefore within the legitimate scope of state intervention. Mill is not committed to accepting the existing scheme of distribution. State intervention to redistribute the wealth and resources of the community does not exceed its proper powers, although it may be condemned on other grounds.

III. CAUSING HARM AND PREVENTING HARM

The extent of Mill's restriction on the scope of social intervention depends on whether intervention is confined to conduct which causes harm to others, or whether it applies much more broadly to cover cases in which intervention prevents harm to others. On the latter, harm-prevention, view, we may interfere with a person's conduct even when the conduct does not cause harm to others, provided only that our interference will prevent harm to others. Mill seems to move from a formulation of his principle in terms of harm-causing to one in terms of harm-prevention.[17] But he needs the broader formulation in terms of harm-prevention in order to cover some of his examples such as 'saving a fellow-creature's life, or interposing to protect the defenceless against ill-usage'. Mill regards failure to save a fellow-creature's life as an omission that causes harm to him. He tries to assimilate omissions to cases of causing harm to others by maintaining, 'A person may cause evil to others not only by this actions but by his inaction, and in either case he is justly accountable to them for the injury.'

But it has been forcefully argued by D. G. Brown[18] that at least in some cases in which I do not save another person's life, or do not protect the defenceless from harm, it does not follow that I cause harm to him. For example, suppose I do not save a drowning person who was pushed into the water by a third party. I may be morally culpable for not saving him, and perhaps I should even be punished for my inaction. But it still does not follow that my inaction is the cause of his drowning, which may be attributed to the third party. So if interference with my liberty will deter others from failing to save drowning people, then it is justifiable — not because my inaction causes harm, but rather because intervention helps to prevent harm to others. To cover this kind of case, Mill would have to accept the wider formulation of his principle to embrace interference to prevent harm to others.[19]

But it has been argued that Mill's whole distinction between self- and other-regarding actions collapses if his principle is expanded in this way. As McCloskey has pointed out, 'A person who fails to help another who is drowning because he is fishing, and the fish biting well, is acting in a purely self-regarding way, even though he thereby allows avoidable harm to come to another.'[20] The force of this objection depends on the assumption that Mill's defence of individual liberty rests on his distinction between two mutually exclusive classes of conduct, self- and other-regarding conduct, and that self-regarding conduct should never be interfered with. However, I have suggested in Chapter 2 that what is really crucial to Mill's case for freedom is not this distinction between different types of conduct, but a different distinction between various reasons for interfering with an individual's conduct. Some reasons for intervention are relevant while others are not. Intervention in order to prevent harm to others is always relevant, but one is never justified in interfering simply because one dislikes the conduct, or strongly disapproves of it. The absoluteness of Mill's barrier against intervention is raised only against certain reasons for intervention which are often invoked.

If we now return to McCloskey's example, we can reply that Mill regarded it as permissible in principle to interfere with a person's fishing, not in order to prohibit that activity, but in order to compel him to save a drowning man, and thereby to prevent harm to others. A person required to save a drowning man may be engaged in any one of a whole variety of different actions, some of which society may disapprove of. If interference with these actions is justified in certain circumstances in order to prevent harm to others, it does not follow that interference is also justified simply in order to prohibit the actions as such. The intervention must always be grounded on the prevention of harm to others, and not on the non-harmful but disapproved-of features of the actions.

Intervention interrupts, but does not prohibit the actions in question.

But how far is Mill prepared to go in allowing intervention to prevent harm to others? Certain constraints on the extent to which one person's welfare may be sacrificed in order to promote the greater welfare of others are imposed by Mill's liberty principle. It does not allow intervention in a person's conduct in order to maximize the general happiness, because the maximization of happiness will go well beyond the prevention of harm to others. But is Mill prepared to accept intervention in order to maximize harm-prevention? This can still involve very great sacrifices of the welfare and liberty of individuals. Consider John Harris's 'survival lottery'.[21] Suppose that two or more patients will die unless they get major organ transplants. They can each acquire the necessary organs from the same person. A method of selecting the unfortunate donor would be to institute a survival lottery which randomly picks out the donor from the whole population. Such a lottery may well maximize harm-prevention because the number of patients who benefit will exceed the number of donors required. What would Mill's attitude be towards such a lottery, and similar schemes for maximizing harm-prevention?

First, the survival lottery is consistent with at least part of Mill's defence of liberty. The lottery does not interfere with conduct simply on the ground that it is disliked or disapproved of by others. If the lottery is properly run, there is no danger that those who offend the moral and religious sensibilities of the majority will be victimized. After all, what really matters is, for example, the condition of the person's heart, and not that of his soul.

Secondly, in *On Liberty* Mill points out that, 'owing to the absence of any recognised principle, liberty is often granted where it should be withheld, as well as withheld where it should be granted.' (p. 159.) So he expects his principled defence of liberty to enlarge liberty in some areas, but to diminish it elsewhere. So perhaps Mill is prepared to choose between schemes of harm-prevention on the basis of purely utilitarian considerations. There are, after all, some utilitarian arguments against the survival lottery,[22] and it may be that there will be very few drastic schemes for harm-prevention which will survive a close utilitarian scrutiny. Would Mill therefore be prepared to leave the case to be settled solely on the balance of conflicting utilitarian considerations? I have some doubts.

These doubts centre on the examples of harm-prevention that Mill envisages. They are all cases in which the cost to the person interfered with is slight compared with the harm to others that is being prevented. The harm prevented is always grave: 'saving a fellow-creature's life, or interposing to protect the defenceless against ill-usage'. In *Utilitarianism* it is again the saving of a life which permits, and indeed makes it a duty 'to steal, or take by force, the necessary food or medicine, or to kidnap, and compel to officiate, the only qualified medical practitioner' (p. 59). In all these cases the interventions to prevent harm do not appear to have major and irreparable adverse effects. Persons called upon to prevent harm to others can resume their activities and pursue their plans of life after the temporary interruptions. Certainly no permanent obstacles are placed to the achievement of their aims and purposes in life. On the other hand, in schemes like the survival lottery, the harm inflicted on any single person can be worse than the harm avoided by each beneficiary of his sacrifice.

Of course an unrestricted policy of maximizing harm-prevention can give rise to all the distributive problems confronting utilitarianism. It will, for example, permit the infliction of the most extreme agony on one person in order to prevent many others from each suffering a very minor harm. Given that the agony suffered by the one person lasts a finite period of time, it will, on the utilitarian calculus, be outweighed by even the smallest harm, spread out over enough people. However, Mill's examples of harm-prevention are confined to cases of grave harm. But the maximization of harm-prevention, even when restricted to cases of grave harm, will still allow for far greater sacrifices of the welfare and freedom of individuals than Mill's examples indicate. Perhaps Mill is trying to restrict the extent of the sacrifices involved when he writes that each person's share 'of the labours and sacrifices incurred for defending the society or its members from injury and molestation' should be fixed 'on some equitable principle'.[23] He does not specify what this 'equitable principle' would be. But as far back as 1832 he already showed an awareness of the need for some fair principle of distribution when he wrote:

Whatever obligation any man would lie under in a state of nature, not to inflict evil upon another for the sake of good to himself, that same obligation lies upon society towards every one of its members. If he injure or molest any of his fellow-citizens, the consequences of whatever they may be obliged to do in self-defence, must fall upon himself; but otherwise, the government fails of its duty, if on any plea of doing good to the community in the aggregate, it reduces him to such a state, that he is on the whole a loser by living in a state of government, and would have been better off if it did not exist. This is the truth which was dimly shadowed forth, in howsoever rude and unskilful a manner, in the theories of the social compact and of the rights of man.[24]

All the little available evidence we have seems to point to an 'equitable principle' in which the sacrifice a person is called upon to make is at least not greater, and perhaps much less, than the harm to each beneficiary. So even here Mill's utilitarianism is tempered by the recognition of some independent principle of distribution.

But Mill's main concern in *On Liberty* is to set limits to intervention in the conduct of individuals. Because of this, once it is clear that certain actions fall within the proper scope of social intervention, he does not usually proceed to discuss further whether intervention is actually justified. He thereby lost the opportunity of formulating more precise general principles for justifying actual intervention. But even so we can draw a few general conclusions from his discussion.

First, permissible interference goes beyond interference with acts of injustice.[25] It is not unjust to fail to save a life because the duty to save a life is not, for Mill, a duty of justice. None the less it may be enforced. Indeed in *Utilitarianism* Mill thinks that this duty is so stringent that it overrides some duties of justice. But he immediately points out that in such cases we tend to re-describe the situation:

. . . as we do not call anything justice which is not a virtue, we usually say, not that justice must give way to some other moral principle, but that what is just in ordinary cases is, by reason of that other principle, not just in the particular case. By this useful accommodation of language, the character of indefeasibility attributed to justice is kept up, and we are saved from the necessity of maintaining that there can be laudable injustice. (p. 59.)

This of course fudges the issue a bit. The special character of the obligations of justice, which Mill is concerned to estab-lish, is destroyed if one is prepared to expand the category of justice to embrace every important moral obligation that should, on a particular occasion, be carried out even when it conflicts with some obligations of justice. Properly described, Mill's position is that a duty of justice may be overridden by another duty of justice, as well as, in some cases, by a moral obligation that is not an obligation of justice.

Secondly, it is a mistake to argue, as has been done recently by D. G. Brown, that 'Distinct and assignable obligations enter, not in determining whose interests are at stake, but in specifying what conduct it is that the weighing of interests will finally justify us in requiring.'[26] Mill's reference to 'distinct and assignable obligations' is made in the context of his reply to the objection that no acts are without some effects on others. Mill acknowledges that every person's conduct can adversely affect others, but he goes on to argue that it is only when the person violates a distinct and assignable obligation to others that 'the case is taken out of the self-regarding class, and becomes amenable to moral disapprobation in the proper sense of the term' (p. 138). His point is not that when a distinct and assignable obligation is violated, the person should actually be interfered with, but rather that there is now a case for intervention as the conduct is taken out of 'the province of liberty'. When he acknowledges that a person's conduct may seriously affect others, he is not thereby claiming that they are harmed. As we have noted in Chapter 2 and earlier in this chapter, he does not count certain kinds of adverse effects on others as constituting harm to them. But violations of distinct and assignable obligations are harmful because they involve breaches of con-tracts or promises.

Finally, in spite of Mill's explicit statement to the contrary, he is sometimes still interpreted as maintaining that the prevention of harm to others is a sufficient condition for the intervention in an individual's conduct.[27] But at the most

Mill's position is that harm to others is a necessary condition for intervention, as when he says: 'it must by no means be supposed that because damage, or probability of damage, to the interests of others, can alone justify the interference of society, that therefore it always does justify such interference.' (p. 150.) Even this may be too strong, and it places pressure on Mill, to which he sometimes yields,[28] to extend his notion of harm in order to cover all the cases where he thinks that intervention is permissible. On one occasion, however, Mill maintains that harm to others provides 'a *prima facie* case' for intervention,[29] and this comes closer to the position he actually defends in *On Liberty*. On the one hand, he wants to rule out certain reasons for intervention: the fact that the action harms the agent, and the fact that the action is disliked by others and regarded as perverse or wrong by them. On the other hand, he treats harm to others as always a good reason, and indeed the central reason, for intervention. But he can maintain both these theses without regarding harm to others as a necessary condition for intervention. For, so long as we retain Mill's relatively narrow notion of harm, there may be other good reasons for intervention, and the two types of reasons with which he was particularly concerned, do not exhaust the whole range of available reasons.

5

Individuality

In Chapter III of *On Liberty* Mill develops and defends the ideal which he describes as that of 'the free development of individuality'.

Individuality is opposed to the blind submission of oneself to the customs and traditions of one's society. Customs may have developed within too narrow a range of experience, and even within that range, what is embodied within customary practices may not be the best interpretation of that experience. Again, the knowledge and wisdom contained in the traditions of one's society may be suited to the needs of ordinary men living in ordinary situations, but not all men are so placed. A particular person may be very different from others, and he may also find himself in highly untypical circumstances. For such a person customary styles of life may have little to offer. Human beings are not machines to be built after a model. They are more like trees which grow and develop from inward forces. Just as not all plants can survive in the same physical atmosphere, so too not all human beings will grow up healthily in the same social atmosphere. Some modes of life will cultivate the potentialities of some individuals, but they will at the same time crush those of others. Different persons require different conditions for their development, and there is no one pattern of life that will suit everybody. The attempt to force, by customary and other pressures, essentially different people into a uniform mould will stunt and warp them, thus preventing them from realizing their different potentialities.

But Mill's central objection to blind conformity to custom is that if a man accepts custom simply because it is custom, then he does not make a choice.[1] To that extent he is less of a human person, for he has failed to develop in himself 'any of the distinctive endowments of a human being' (p. 116). These distinctive human faculties of 'perception, judgment, discriminative feeling, mental activity, and even moral preference, are exercised only in making a choice' (p. 116). Those

who are unable or who refuse to exercise their human capacity
for choice, Mill compares with apes, with cattle, with sheep,
and with steam-engines. They have lost or surrendered that
which is distinctively human, that which marks them out
from the rest of nature and from the artefacts of human
creation which cannot have aims and purposes of their own
but are designed by human beings to serve the purposes of
human beings. Once one has succeeded in building a good
machine for a particular purpose, one can multiply it many
times, and each additional machine, so long as it is a faithful
copy of the original, will be just as good as the original. But
with human beings the matter is different. Even with human
beings who are very similar in potentialities, and who are
similarly placed, it is not the case that they would all have
the same human worth if they were all forced to copy a
good model of their kind. It is possible that a person 'might
be guided in some good path, and kept out of harm's way'
without his making choices of his own. 'But what will be his
comparative worth as a human being? It really is of importance, not only what men do, but also what manner of men
they are that do it.' (p. 117.) What is lost in the forced imitation by human beings of good models of conduct is the
conscious choice between alternatives, and all that this
involves. The act of choice brings into play various faculties.

He who chooses his plan for himself employs all his faculties. He must
use observation to see, reasoning and judgment to foresee, activity to
gather materials for decision, discrimination to decide, and when he has
decided, firmness and self-control to hold to his deliberate decision.
And these qualities he requires and exercises exactly in proportion as
the part of his conduct which he determines according to his own
judgment and feelings is a large one. (p. 117.)

Men who make choices develop what Mill calls a 'character':
their desires and feelings are the products of their own
conscious choices and are not the passively generated products
of external factors.

Individuality for Mill, therefore, consists in part in the
readiness to make deliberate and considered choices between
alternative beliefs and patterns of life, and in part in the
direction and content of such choices. The right choice for
each individual depends on the sort of person he is, and hence

varies from individual to individual. Each person should choose that pattern of life which develops to the fullest extent his potentialities, subject only to the condition that in so developing himself, he does not harm others, and so does not hamper their development. Mill does not go further to specify how one can discover what one's potentialities are. He believes that freedom and variety of situations are the necessary conditions for this discovery.

A common criticism of Mill's notion of individuality is that he equates mere eccentricity with individuality. This point of view is well put by R. P. Anschutz who accuses Mill of substituting 'bohemian nonsense for bourgeois nonsense'.[2] Mill, he says, is guilty of 'the error of assuming that a man is only himself when he succeeds in being different from other men, as if individuality meant peculiarity and idiosyncracy. Hence — and this is the greatest weakness of his position — he is led to ignore the fundamental part played by tradition in providing a context for the empty form of individuality.'[3] But the objection is mistaken. Mill is not opposed to tradition and custom as such. Either to reject or accept customary practices, without first considering their claims as opposed to those of alternative patterns of behaviour, is equally to refuse to exercise choice. In fact Mill believes that there is much that men may learn from the customs of their society. To reject them out of hand is foolish, for customs embody past experience which may well be relevant to the present problems of many men. Customary practices can furnish useful guides as to how we should choose, but it is the necessity for choice from which we should not run away. If a person, in exercising choice, decides that a customary style of life is the one that most suits him, there is nothing that Mill need find objectionable. However, at the time when he wrote, he felt that the sway of custom was too great. There was a 'despotism of custom', and this was manifested in two different ways in which the lives of men were affected. First, the demands of custom were imposed on many. Men were forced to act in the same way and to hold the same beliefs. Second, even when customary rules were not imposed, men willingly and unthinkingly accepted them. It never occurred to them that there could be alternative ways of doing things. Mill praises eccentricity in this context because it is a means of breaking through the tyranny of custom. Eccentricity provokes thought. It shows men that alternative ways of life are possible. It shakes men out of their unthinking complacency, and thereby encourages them to accept or reject custom as an act of conscious choice. His hostility toward the uniformity of human behaviour should also not be taken as an expression of his love of variety and eccentricity as such. He in fact believes that human beings are different from one another, and that if they were allowed to pursue their own plans of life, individuals would behave differently. Uniformity of behaviour is an artificial state of affairs created by the tyranny of prevailing fashions. Uniformity of human behaviour is therefore for him a sign that human nature has been suppressed and forced into a narrow range of preconceived directions and patterns. Certain avenues of self-development have been blocked. So he values variety and eccentricity not in themselves but because he believes that the free development of individuality will in fact produce variety and eccentricity in human conduct, and these are welcomed as expressions of individuality.

The ideal of individuality is one that Mill thinks is within the reach of all men, and it is therefore not an élitist notion. But here, as elsewhere, he sees a special role for the élite. He believes that only a few men are capable of *initiating* new practices. The rest are, however, capable of realizing their individualities too because they can choose for themselves among a range of alternatives which they have not initiated. Like so many other political thinkers, Mill sees the prevailing state of human affairs as highly undesirable and the life of men in such a state as lacking in dignity. But unlike many other thinkers, he does not put forward an authoritarian solution. He relies in the end on the processes of reasoning and on the therapeutic shocks to complacency which new ways of life are likely to have. To force ignorant and complacent men to realize their individuality is for him a contradiction. The element of free choice is necessary, though not sufficient. So the élite have only 'the freedom to point out the way', but not the right to coerce others. 'The power of compelling others into it is not only inconsistent with the freedom and development of all the rest, but corrupting to the strong man himself.' (p. 124.) Here he displays the characteristic liberal fear of the corrupting effects of vesting too much power in the hands of men, no matter how enlightened or morally good they may be. The élite should persuade others not to remain in their present undesirable state and should set examples of how men may 'grow up to the mental, moral, and aesthetic stature of which their nature is capable' (p. 125).

The significance of Mill's notion of individuality is that he has in fact paved a middle way between the doctrines of Benthamite utilitarianism and those of later British idealist philosophers. A Benthamite utilitarian is not primarily concerned with how people come to have certain desires; he takes men's existing desires as the given data, and he concerns himself with trying to satisfy as many of these desires as possible in such a way that the greatest amount of happiness is produced. The idealist philosophers, on the other hand, are more interested in what a man ought to do than in what he currently desires to do. A man's true self is taken to be a rational self, and not the person we meet every day. When Mill speaks of the importance of having a 'character' and of cultivating desires of 'home growth', or of desires that have grown out of one's free choices, he is very much concerned to provide a basis for the criticism of the existing desires of men and of the way in which they come to engage in various activities. The barriers to freedom of thought and action are not exhausted in prisons and in threats of punishment, all those things that combine to prevent a person from carrying out what he wishes to do. In a closed society where the sources of information are very limited, and only prevailing views are easily accessible, men tend to come under the unquestioning sway of these views. They do not hold views different from the prevailing ones or seek to conduct them-selves differently from customary practices. There is, therefore, no need for them to be restrained by threats of punishment and by prison bars. Yet such men are, as Mill would say, in a state of 'mental slavery', unaware of and therefore uncon-cerned with alternative conceptions of what is worth doing, or of what is true or desirable. They remain conditioned and docile creatures without any beliefs and desires which are the products of the deliberate choices they have made. They have merely passively assimilated what is in their limited social environment.

Mill's emphasis is on the cultivation of active rather than passive persons. Men are not to be viewed simply as passive instruments for the reform and reconstruction of society by a few enlightened men: 'there are as many independent centres of improvement as there are individuals.' (p. 128.) The plea for individuality is also a plea for a society that is open to a variety of influences and ideas and that does not seek to control and manipulate knowledge, for it is only in such a society that men can discover what they really regard as valuable and important and what views and plans of life they are prepared to accept. To take the existing views and desires of men as the ultimate basis of political calculation, without regard to the way in which these views are formed, is to surrender to the tyranny of current orthodoxies. On the other hand, to disregard such views and desires completely, and to seek to impose enlightened standards on all against their clear wishes, is to practise paternalism. Mill's ideal of individuality provides an alternative to these two influential traditions of social and political thought.

What is the connection between freedom and individuality? As we have seen, individuality *consists* in part of choosing for oneself. Hence the connection between freedom and individuality is internal. There seems to be a similar relation between individuality and some kinds of happiness. Mill is of course well known for his claim that 'some *kinds* of pleasure are more desirable and more valuable than others.'[4] The connection between individuality and happiness depends on the kinds of pleasure one has in mind. As far as the qualitatively lower pleasures are concerned, the connection is purely contingent. But Mill seems to envisage a more intimate connection between individuality and some of the qualitatively higher pleasures. Thus he urges men to cultivate 'native pleasures', or the pleasures of 'home growth', pleasures that are linked to the making of free choices between alternative patterns of life (p. 119). These 'native pleasures' cannot be attained except through the pursuit of individuality and the exercise of freedom that it involves. Indeed Mill sometimes

gives the impression that these pleasures are identical with
the exercise of free choice, though in general he adopts the
position that free choice is a logically necessary condition
for their attainment. His view seems to be that the native
pleasures consist in the enjoyment of activities which one has
freely and critically chosen from a range of alternatives.

We are now in a position to understand Mill's sense of
utility 'grounded on the permanent interest of man as a
progressive being'. Liberty is necessary for 'the free development of individuality', and without liberty 'there is wanting
one of the principal ingredients of human happiness, and
quite the chief ingredient of individual and social progress.'
(p. 115.) Thus Mill is still appealing to utility, or the promotion of happiness as the standard for appraising the value of
liberty. He also claims that because of the diversity of the
sources of human pleasures and pains, and their different
effects on different persons, men will 'neither obtain their
fair share of happiness, nor grow up to the mental, moral and
aesthetic stature of which their nature is capable' unless they
are allowed freedom to pursue their own modes of life (p. 125).
It becomes clear as the argument proceeds, that the ultimate
goal is not really happiness in any sense that is detachable
from the growth of individuality. 'Utility in the largest sense'
refers to the development of individuality and its associated
pleasures. Liberty is to be valued because it is a logically
necessary condition for the growth of individuality. Men
must be allowed to choose for themselves because free choice
is itself a most important ingredient of the kind of happiness
Mill was most concerned to promote. Men who choose in
conformity with custom, not because they independently
agree with it, but blindly and without thought, or because
they are pressured to do so, cannot by definition be happier
than those who choose freely. Happiness of this kind is not
what Bentham conceived — a goal that is distinct from
individual liberty, and as a matter of fact achievable through
it in certain situations.[5] For Mill, happiness is not something
that can be got through any means. It is not just what men
believe or how they feel which is important; the manner in
which they come to have certain beliefs and attitudes is also
important. 'If a person possesses any tolerable amount of

common sense and experience, his own mode of laying down
his existence is the best, not because it is best in itself, but
because it is his own mode.' (p. 125.) The importance of
choosing and acting independently and in a rational manner
is further emphasized by the use of expressions like 'an
intellectually active people' and 'the dignity of thinking
beings'. Rational choice, as Mill's arguments in the chapter
on freedom of thought and discussion make clear, implies
that one knows the correct grounds for believing something,
and that one is prepared to listen to conflicting views whenever they arise. It thus implies the existence of freedom for
those who disagree with us.

Although Mill attaches great intrinsic value to the development of individuality, he also points out that the growth
of individuality will produce good consequences. This is of
course perfectly consistent, for something can be valued both
as an end in itself and as a means to some other end. Mill
complains that 'individual spontaneity is hardly recognized
by the common modes of thinking as having any intrinsic
worth, or deserving any regard on its own account.' (p. 115.)
It is for this reason that Mill thinks it important to show how
the development of individuality in one person can be of use
to others who do not value their own individuality. The
ordinary person would not be very impressed by an account
of individuality which merely extols its intrinsic value, and
this is why Mill's defence takes the form it does of spelling
out both the intrinsic and instrumental values of individuality.[6]

Having said that the individuality is the same thing as development, and
that it is only the cultivation of individuality which produces, or can
produce, well-developed human beings, I might here close the argument:
for what more or better can be said of any condition of human affairs
than that it brings human beings themselves nearer to the best thing
they can be? or what worse can be said of any obstruction to good than
that it prevents this? Doubtless, however, these considerations will not
suffice to convince those who most need convincing; and it is necessary
further to show, that these developed human beings are of some use to
the undeveloped — to point out to those who do not desire liberty, and
would not avail themselves of it, that they may be in some intelligible
manner rewarded for allowing other people to make use of it without
hindrance. (pp. 121–2.)

Mill goes on to argue that everybody benefits from progress and improvement which depends on new ideas, the introduction of more enlightened conduct, and the cultivation of new tastes and styles of living.

In a recent paper,[7] James Bogen and Daniel Farrell suggest that Mill's claim that freedom and individuality are intrinsically desirable is fully compatible with his utilitarianism which regards happiness as the only thing intrinsically desirable. According to them, by happiness Mill does not simply mean a mental state, but also, and more importantly, the set of all those things which are intrinsically desirable. When Mill treats pleasure or happiness as a mental state, he regards happiness in this sense as just one of the things that are intrinsically desirable. But Mill also regards many other things which are not mental states as intrinsically desirable. For example, money, health, and virtue are desirable as ends. It is not the mental states produced by these objects and activities which are intrinsically desirable, but the objects and activities themselves. So if happiness is a collection of all the intrinsically desirable goods, then liberty and individuality can be included in this collection.

Bogen and Farrell interpret Mill as claiming in *Utilitarianism* that 'what is desired as an end is desirable as an end.'[8] Mill believes that 'Whatever is desired otherwise than as a means to some end beyond itself, and ultimately to happiness, is desired as itself a part of happiness, and is not desired for itself until it has become so.'[9] But Bogen and Farrell argue that Mill is only committed to the view that a thing's production of pleasure (as a mental state) is a causally necessary and sufficient condition for our desiring that thing for its own sake. For example, the intrinsically desirable sight of a snow-capped mountain gleaming in the moonlight may be for some both a necessary and sufficient condition for their having a desire to climb the mountain. But once they have the desire to climb, this desire could be an end in itself and not simply a means to catching another glimpse of the mountain.[10] Similarly, virtue could be desired and desirable for its own sake, even though it was originally desired simply as a means to pleasure (as a mental state). It could be desired even if it no longer produced pleasure.

The crucial question is whether the account just given shows that Mill's defence of freedom and individuality is, as Bogen and Farrell claim, 'a straightforwardly utilitarian defence'.[11] They themselves draw attention to the problem of deciding how to resolve conflicts between different ends. Since a plurality of ends, or intrinsically desirable goods, is subsumed under the notion of happiness, Mill would have to determine the order of priority between these ends in cases of conflict. Even though they think that the principle of utility itself cannot resolve the ordering problem,[12] Bogen and Farrell do not seem to think that this affects the utilitarian character of Mill's defence of liberty. But unless there are utilitarian reasons for ranking one value higher than another, the utilitarian cannot consistently accept that ranking. Unless liberty and the development of individuality maximize happiness or the net satisfaction of desires, there is no basis for the utilitarian to accord them the highest value. There is of course no reason why utilitarianism should be tied to the notion of happiness as a mental state.[13] But at the same time whatever notion of happiness one employs in formulating utilitarianism cannot be such as to make the doctrine indistinguishable from rival non-utilitarian theories.[14] For then the claim that Mill's defence of liberty is a straightforwardly utilitarian defence would be empty. The arguments of Bogen and Farrell are inconclusive precisely because they leave off at this crucial point.

Until we have a clearer picture of how liberty and individuality rank in Mill's order of priorities, and the reasons for the ranking, we cannot claim that he is a straightforward utilitarian. Indeed there are a few obstacles in Mill's defence of individuality to the establishment of this claim. Just as, on the account given by Bogen and Farrell, liberty is intrinsically desirable because it is desired as an end by some people, many other people desire for their own sakes general comformity and the suppression of deviant conduct. For a utilitarian, the intensity of a desire and the number of people who share it will affect the value to be attached to its satisfaction. But Mill's awareness of the widespread existence and strength of these anti-liberal desires did not lead him to give them any additional weight. Nor did it weaken for him the intrinsic value of individuality. Mill did not believe that the degree of desirability of something is proportional to the extent to which it is actually desired as an end. He placed a high intrinsic value on individuality in the full knowledge that there was too little appreciation of it, and too little desire for it.[15]

But it will of course be claimed that in the long run the promotion of liberty and individuality will lead to the greater satisfaction of desires than the imposition of conformity and the exercise of coercion. But even if this is true, it gives a misleading account of Mill's position. First, in discussing self-regarding conduct, we saw that Mill wished to discount certain satisfactions and certain forms of distress in his calculation. It is just because he disregarded certain satisfactions that he could be so sure that the over-all consequences of developing individuality would indeed be favourable. Secondly, it is also the case that the high intrinsic value he placed on individuality did not depend on the degree of satisfaction it yielded, but on its development of certain capacities. And the development of these capacities is valued in itself and not as a means to the satisfaction of desires. In a brief but valuable discussion, R. S. Downie has suggested that Mill's qualitative distinction between pleasures can be restated as a distinction between activities: 'a higher value can be set on some activities than on others, not for the amount of pleasure they produce but for their ability to deepen a person's individuality and so help him to develop himself.'[16] It is self-development, and not the mere satisfaction of desire, that Mill valued. Some of those who do not develop their individuality have strong desires to conform unthinkingly to a certain way of life. Mill believed that their desires should be satisfied so long as there is no harm to others, but he did not place a high value on the satisfaction of these desires.

From the utilitarian point of view it is also puzzling that Mill should insist so uncompromisingly that individuality be developed within 'the limits imposed by the rights and interests of others', and that he should so absolutely refuse to allow anyone, including 'the strong man of genius' to develop himself at the cost of the individuality of others. Utilitarianism, as an aggregative doctrine, will seek to maximize the sum of intrinsic value. If individuality has intrinsic value, then, other things being equal, this involves maximizing the realization of individuality. But maximization may involve the sacrifice of the individuality of some in order to promote a net increase in the realization of the individuality of the rest.[17] In *A Theory of Justice*, Rawls argues that Mill can be rescued from this only by making assumptions analogous to those relied on by utilitarians.[18] Thus Mill would have to assume that individuals have a similar capacity to develop individuality, and that the right to liberty has diminishing marginal utility. He can then maintain that a person who has already exercised to some degree his right to liberty by developing his individuality, will promote individuality to a lesser extent than another person who has not yet exercised this right. With these assumptions we can explain why maximum intrinsic value will be promoted by the granting of an equal liberty to all to develop individuality.

However, there is no need for Mill to make these assumptions because his doctrine of individuality does not imply a maximization of the realization of individuality. Distributive requirements are already built into his doctrine. His liberty principle restricts interference with a person's freedom to cases where harm to others can be prevented. Failure to realize one's own individuality is not a harm to others, whereas the suppression of another person's individuality is a form of harmful conduct — an unwarranted interference with his freedom. So to suppress a person's freedom in order to promote the individuality of others is to harm him without any justification in terms of harm-prevention. By the same token, to cultivate one's individuality by harming others violates the liberty principle. Thus the prevention of harm to others sets limits both to what may be done to help others realize their individuality, and to what may be done to realize one's own individuality. Within these limits, Mill hopes that *each* person will, with the help of others, develop his individuality to the fullest.

Mill's claim that freedom and individuality are important as ends in themselves has often been misunderstood. It is not the claim that all freely chosen acts are good or valuable, nor does it imply that there is some value in an immoral act

simply in virtue of its being freely chosen.[19] Mill also does
not deny that good consequences can flow from coerced and
unfree acts. His emphasis is on the worth of the *agent* — 'his
comparative worth as a human being' (p. 117). Freedom is
a precondition of the worth of the agent, and an essential
component in his ideal of individuality. Unless a person's
actions are freely chosen, he cannot be regarded as a worthy
person, even though good results may have been achieved by
the denial of his freedom.

What is the relation between the acceptance of freedom
as an end in the sense advocated by Mill, and the belief in
objective truths? This is an issue that has been excellently
discussed by Basil Mitchell.[20] He distinguishes between
different varieties of liberalism, and in particular between
what may be called 'the old liberalism', which claims that
only in a free society will men be able to discover true answers
to moral and other related questions, and what he calls 'the
new liberalism', which values freedom because it denies that
there are objective truths. According to Mitchell, the new
liberalism is represented by P. F. Strawson in his paper,
'Social Morality and Individual Ideal',[21] where he argues
for the freedom of individuals to bring into effect a variety
of different and conflicting ideals of life within the framework of a common social morality. Freedom is valued not
on the ground that it is the best, or perhaps even the only,
means of promoting the discovery of new truths, for the
new liberal does not believe that there is a truth about life;
but rather freedom is valued because it promotes ethical
diversity which is regarded as intrinsically good. On the other
hand, according to Mitchell, Mill is an advocate of the old
liberalism although 'the seeds of the new liberalism' are to
be found in his defence of individuality. Mill never embraces
fully the new liberalism because, even when he praises individuality, he is not indifferent to the question of truth. He
sees the importance of individuality in the discovery of new
truths that it makes possible, and in setting the example of
'more enlightened conduct and better taste and sense in life'.[22]
With Mill as the notable exception, Mitchall argues that there
is in general a tension between the belief that one already has
the truth and the belief in the importance of freedom. So

those who claim that there are objective truths, already known, feel constrained to deny toleration, while those who wish to vindicate freedom feel obliged to deny objectivity. However, a middle path between the old and the new liberalism is possible: there is 'a liberal case which does not rest on the premise that the truth is not known or not knowable'. This case rests on the belief that 'a man cannot live the life of a moral and rational being unless he is able to make his own choices, so that restriction of his power by fear of punishment is in itself an evil.'[23]

But if my account of Mill's doctrine of individuality is correct, then Mitchell's middle path lies in the very heart of Mill's case for freedom. Mill of course also subscribes to some version of the old liberalism, as is shown by his argument that freedom of expression leads to the discovery of truth and the elimination of error.[24] There is no inconsistency here, for Mill recognizes that freedom has instrumental value and is also to be valued as an end in itself. The old liberalism merely captured the instrumental value of freedom. On the other hand, the significance of freedom as an end is given expression in both the new liberalism and in Mitchell's middle way. In saying that Mill subscribes to the latter rather than to the former, it is still necessary to account for 'the seeds of the new liberalism' to which Mitchell alluded.

There is first no necessary incompatibility between the new liberalism and the middle path. What is distinctive of the middle path is that, unlike the new liberalism, it does not *presuppose* the absence of objective truths. But this is quite compatible with there being *in fact* no objective truths. Whereas the new liberalism collapses if there are objective truths, the middle way remains equally viable whether or not there are in fact such truths.

Mill believes that there are objective truths in many areas, and his discussion of freedom of expression makes this clear. But in the area of personal ideals concerning the sort of life a person should lead, or the sort of person he should strive to be, his view is complex, and it is here that the seeds of the new liberalism seem to be sown.

It is, however, very odd to claim in the alleged spirit of the new liberalism that there is an area of life where it is a matter of indifference to what ideals one subscribes. One may indeed, as Strawson says, experience sympathy 'with a variety of conflicting ideals of life', but I doubt that he wants this to be taken as suggesting that one sympathizes with every ideal of life that men happen to accept, or that they may be persuaded to accept. One's sympathy extends to a certain range of conflicting ideals, and within that range, no question about one ideal being truer or better arises. But there is, or should be, a limit beyond which ideals of life are rejected because they are regarded as degrading, or because they do violence to one's general conceptions of what human life should be.

It is against this background that Mill's notion of individuality can be further elucidated. Within a certain range Mill undoubtedly accepts different ideals of life as equally valid for different men.

There is no reason that all human existence should be constructed on some one or some small number of patterns . . . Such are the differences among human beings in their sources of pleasure, their susceptibilities of pain, and the operation on them of different physical and moral agencies, that unless there is a corresponding diversity in their modes of life, they neither obtain their fair share of happiness, nor grow up to the mental, moral, and aesthetic stature of which their nature is capable. (p. 125.)

This sounds like the new liberalism, but Mill's range of sympathy is not unrestricted. He still recoils for example, from the ideal of polygamous marriages which he views with deep disapprobation and as 'a retrograde step in civilisation' (p. 148). The institution of polygamy falls outside his range of what is attractive or captivating, though not of course outside his range of what should be tolerated.

More generally, it may be said that to the question, what sort of life a person should lead or what sort of person he should become, Mill does not believe that there is one objectively true answer applicable to all men. But at the same time he does not think that so long as the agent's choice is freely and deliberately made, it is to be welcomed no matter what its content may be. The free and deliberate choice of a way of life is only one component in his ideal of individuality. The other component is that the choice should be such as to develop a person's potentialities. Now no matter how different the potentialities of different persons may be, there are still some basic resemblances between them simply in virtue of the fact that they are human beings. They have 'the distinctive human endowments', and it is part of every man's potentialities to develop these endowments.[25] Depending on what their other and more specific potentialities are, different men will find different plans of life most conducive to their self-development. But certain limits are set to the type of conduct which will be compatible with the ideal of individuality. For if a chosen plan of life is such as to destroy to a large extent, or to arrest the growth of these endowments, it would retard a person's potentialities, and hence run foul of Mill's second component of individuality.

Again, a person may also fail to develop fully his more specific potentialities, his special talents and abilities, because of a lack of knowledge and guidance. The traditions of one's society and the experience of others can therefore be very helpful if only they are taken account of intelligently. But changing circumstances call for adjustments in one's plan of life. What may have been an ideal form of life for a certain type of person under one set of circumstances may cease to be so when new circumstances arise. Hence, 'There is always need of persons not only to discover new truths, and point out when what were once truths are true no longer, but also to commence new practices, and set the example of more enlightened conduct, and better taste and sense in human life.' (p. 122.) For a variety of reasons. Mill cannot be indifferent to the question of truth, and must therefore subscribe to Mitchell's middle way rather than to the new liberalism. None the less he seems to come closer to the new liberalism when he is putting the case for individuality than when he is arguing for freedom of expression, and this calls for some explanation.

In defending individuality, Mill is concerned with those personal ideals of life which, if they are carried out, do not cause harm to others, whereas in discussing the case for freedom of expression he emphasizes inter-personal questions of concern to all about what is right or wrong, true or false, good or bad in 'morals, religion, politics, social relations and the business of life'. Many of these latter issues are about our common social duties and responsibilities, the merits and demerits of social institutions, and the pursuit of appropriate social policies. In these areas the analogy with choosing a coat or a pair of boots (p. 125), which Mill uses in the context of personal ideals, is inapplicable. The correct answers in these areas do not vary, as they do in the case of personal ideals, with the individuals to whom we are speaking: it would be inappropriate to say here that a size of boots or a coat which fits perfectly well one person would not fit another.

Mill believes that freedom and variety of situations are indispensable conditions for the flowering of individuality. Freedom is necessary because individuality consists in part of choosing for oneself. Variety of situations is necessary because the genuineness of one's choice is to a great extent dependent on the range of alternatives one can visualize. Though it is of course possible for a man who has not been presented with alternative beliefs and modes of life to conceive such modes and to reject them critically in favour of the way of life prevailing in his society, this possibility is considerably reduced for most men if they do not have the opportunity of knowing about 'experiments in living', or of listening to and reading about views which propose such alternatives. Variety of situations enlarges the range of alternatives available for choice, and also puts alternatives more vividly before us.

Individuality does not, however, exhaust the goals of political action. A good society will pursue other goals apart from the promotion of each person's individuality. But the ideal of individuality guides the manner in which these other goals are to be reached. The framework of political life is set by this ideal, and the pursuit of other goals is to be carried out within this framework. Mill's liberalism does not seek to provide solutions to every contemporary political problem. But individuality furnishes a positive guide to political action in two ways. At a rather general level, it sets limits to what may be done in the attainment of other goals. It is not an ideal that is to be put aside while we get down to the business of seeking other things. Secondly, it itself makes more specific claims by insisting that opportunities for its realization should be provided. Non-interference with a person's conduct except to prevent harm to others is important. So is the protection and improvement of the institutions which allow and encourage free discussion where they already exist, and the building up of these institutions where they do not yet exist. The creation and maintenance of an atmosphere of toleration constitute a permanent part of the aims of political action.

6

Enforcing Shared Values

A persistent criticism of Mill's liberty principle is its alleged failure to recognize that there are certain important social structures and institutions which a society is justified in protecting even at the cost of coercing individuals whose conduct threatens to undermine them. The most notable recent attempt to support this point of view is by Lord Devlin in his much discussed book, *The Enforcement of Morals*,[1] in which he explicitly picks on Mill as one of his main targets of attack. Devlin's argument centres on what he regards as the vital function of the criminal law in enforcing the generally shared moral values of a society which are associated with its important institutions. The case for the law's enforcement of society's shared morality is based on several different considerations, most of which are embodied in two doctrines which Hart has labelled the 'disintegration thesis' and the 'conservative thesis' respectively.[2] According to the disintegration thesis, a shared morality is what holds a society together, and hence the enforcement of this morality is necessary to prevent society from collapsing, or at least weakening. On the other hand, the conservative thesis maintains that 'the majority have a right to follow their moral convictions that their moral environment is a thing of value to be defended from change.'[3] In this chapter I shall discuss each of these theses in turn, and determine the extent to which they are incompatible with Mill's liberty principle.

I. DEVLIN'S DISINTEGRATION THESIS

In putting forward his disintegration thesis, Devlin argues that a society's existence depends on the maintenance of shared political and moral values. Violation of the shared morality loosens one of the bonds which hold a society together, and thereby threatens it with disintegration. The criminal law may therefore be invoked to protect this shared morality in the same way as it is used against treason and sedition.[4] Breaches of the shared morality do not cause harm to other individuals in the way that murder and assault do, but none the less they harm *society* by undermining its moral structure. Even acts like homosexuality between consenting adults in private can threaten the existence of society, and therefore society has the right to suppress them.

However, there are certain 'elastic' principles which determines when society should exercise this right.[5] As far as possible there should be toleration of individual liberty. The law should also be slow to act in enforcing moral standards, in case the strong feelings against a particular form of conduct should subside and deprive the law of the backing it needs to be effective. Again, privacy should be respected wherever possible. Finally, the law may not be a suitable instrument for upholding all the shared values of a society.

But Devlin believes that 'the limits of tolerence' are reached when the feelings of the ordinary person towards a particular form of conduct reaches a certain intensity of 'intolerance, indignation and disgust'. If, for example, it is the genuine feeling of society that homosexuality is 'a vice so abominable that its mere presence is an offence',[6] then society may eradicate it.

Devlin believes that violations of the shared morality result in two types of harm to society — tangible and intangible.

The 'tangible harm' seems to consist in a diminution of the physical strength of society. There are activities which are quite harmless to society when only a few of its members indulge in them, but which become harmful when the number of participants grows large. Devlin cites drunkenness as an example. He also argues that 'unrestricted indulgence in vice' will weaken an individual to the extent that he ceases to be a useful member of society, and society itself will be weakened if it has a sufficient number of such weak members.[7] He believes that a vicious minority 'diminishes the physical strength of society'.[8] Here then is one sense in which violation of the shared morality harms society: society loses its physical strength because immorality breeds physical weakness in its members.

But the argument here does not fit in very well with Devlin's general account of the importance of having a shared morality.

The tangible harm that certain forms of conduct allegedly cause is not related to the fact that such conduct breaches the shared morality. For if drunkenness, drug-taking, and fornication are physically weakening, then they are so quite independently of whether they violate the shared morality of society. Devlin believes that the cohesiveness of the shared morality does not depend on its quality, but on the fact that it is commonly accepted by the members of the society.[9] This being the case, it is quite possible that the debaucheries of one society would form part of the cherished shared morality of another society. Do they then cease to be physically weakening? If, for example, fornication is physically weakening, then surely it remains so even if it becomes acceptable to the shared morality of society. But if, on the other hand, it is the 'unrestricted indulgence' in sexual activities which is physically weakening, then it is difficult to understand what difference it makes when such indulgence takes place within marriage rather than outside it. Of course it may be that the physical weakness stems from attempts to evade apprehension by the law. But in that case the remedy is simply to remove the sanctions of the law.

Again, drinking, drug-taking, homosexuality, abortion, and suicide may cause serious social problems if they are widely and indiscriminately practised. But so also would birth control, or the very different practice of having very large families, or even, as Devlin himself acknowledges,[10] celibacy. It is therefore not *qua* breaches of the shared morality that certain activities can become harmful to society, and hence their being harmful does not in any way support Devlin's disintegration thesis.

But Devlin also postulates a second type of harm caused by deviations from the shared morality of society. This is what he calls the 'intangible harm' resulting from the weakening of the commonly held moral beliefs. Most men, he claims, take their morality as a whole, and immoral activity, by weakening belief in one part of society's shared morality, will probably result in the undermining of the whole morality. When there ceases to be common belief in the value of the moral code, society is threatened with disintegration. Whatever is involved in the 'disintegration' of society, on this argument it is brought about via the rejection of the shared morality.

Devlin stresses that he is not against change as such in the shared morality. But he points out that an existing shared morality cannot be quickly replaced by another shared morality in the way that one changes an old coat for a new one.[11] There will first be a long period in which common moral beliefs are absent. It is this 'interregnum' which is dangerous. But against this it can be argued that the whole of the existing shared morality is not under threat at the same time. At any one time only parts of the shared morality will be changed, or will be challenged, and there will be other parts which will be sufficiently accepted to ensure the safety and cohesiveness of society. Devlin rejects this possibility because he believes in the connectedness of the different parts of the shared morality. On his view, if one undermines one part of the shared morality, one threatens the whole of that shared morality. He does not explain why he thinks that the shared morality should be connected in this, rather than in another way, nor does he cite evidence in support of his claim.[12]

But suppose that the available evidence is indecisive as between various alternative accounts of the shared morality. Where then does the burden of proof lie? It has been suggested that societies can only be guided by their own lights. If, in a particular society, there is a genuine belief in the disintegration thesis, then this would be adequate justification for Devlin's position.[13] On this view, if, for example, it is generally believed that deviations from the shared sexual morality will bring about the collapse of society, then this is sufficient to justify the suppression of the deviant conduct. But no one with even a minimal respect for individual freedom can possibly accept this. Religious intolerance, racial persecution, and the suppression of the fundamental liberties of minorities, can all be justified on this basis. The belief that tolerance and freedom lead to the collapse of society need not then be supported by evidence. A person may conduct his own life according to his own lights, but where one is going to inflict suffering on others and deprive them of their valued freedom for the sake of avoiding a very speculative harm, one must surely accept the burden of proof.

Devlin's 'elastic' principles show that he has a general respect for tolerance and individual freedom. But at the same time he rejects Mill's defence of freedom because he thinks that Mill works with too idealistic a picture of human beings. He claims that Mill envisages people earnestly and conscientiously doing what they think is right even though others disapprove of their conduct. But this is seldom true of those who violate the shared morality of society. Devlin thinks that most of them acknowledge the wrongness of their conduct, but still act as they do because of lust and the desire for money. He declares: 'Freedom to do what you know to be bad is worthless.'[14]

But Devlin's argument is not persuasive, and his dichotomy of human motivation is too simple. A person may violate the generally accepted values of his society not because he is too weak to refrain from an action he knows to be wrong, but rather because he believes that in those areas many different modes of conduct are morally permissible. In areas where conduct does not harm others, it is quite common for a person to think that what should be done varies with one's tastes, temperament, and personality. Such a person may not wish to win anyone over to the way of life he has chosen for himself because it is not the only one he regards as acceptable, and it may not suit others. But equally, he does not believe that what he does it wrong, and he would certainly strongly resent any interference. It is much easier to see this point of view if one moves away from the emotionally charged sexual sphere to the choice of hair-styles, clothes, food, drinks, houses, cars, hobbies, etc. In all these cases one may, at least to a certain degree, be indulging oneself, but where such indulgence is not regarded as wrong, there is not strong reason for the person to avoid pleasing himself. Many forms of conduct which Devlin regards as vices are not acknowledged as such by those who engage in them. No doubt such acts are not done out of a deep conviction that they are the uniquely right acts to perform, or for the sake of Queen and country, but simply because they are regarded as enjoyable. A great deal of human freedom is demanded for the sake of being able to engage in such innocuous activities.

Devlin does not succeed in providing good grounds for the

acceptance of his disintegration thesis. But even if the thesis is true, how does it undermine Mill's liberty principle? Devlin writes of harm to society as opposed to harm to individuals. Perhaps he is here invoking something like Feinberg's distinction between 'the public harm principle' and 'the private harm principle'.[15] On this account 'harm to individuals' is constituted by injury to specific individuals such as is caused by acts of homicide, assault, and robbery. On the other hand, 'public harm' consists of the 'impairment of institutional practices and regulatory systems that are in the public interest'.[16] Feinberg suggests that Devlin's disintegration thesis, with its appeal to the notion of harm to society, is really an application of the public harm principle that coercion necessary to prevent public harm is justifiable.[17] If this is the case, then there is no disagreement of principle between Devlin and Mill, for Mill' notion of harm, as explicated in Chapter 4, embraces both private and public harm. If the factual claims made by Devlin are correct, then even on Mill's liberty principle there is a case for the legal enforcement of the shared morality. For on this interpretation of Devlin's disintegration thesis, the harm which justifies legal intervention is not identical with the mere feelings of 'intolerance, indignation and disgust' which are aroused when the majority in a society learn that their deeply cherished moral values have been breached. Rather the presence of these feelings become a *sign* of impending harm if deviations from the shared morality are left unchecked. However, when one moves from his disintegration to his conservative thesis, the notion of public harm is either dropped, or else it is transformed in such a manner as to be indistinguishable from the mere feelings of intolerance, indignation, and disgust in the majority. In either case the conservative thesis is incompatible with Mill's liberty principle. But that is a matter to be explored a little later. Confining ourselves to Devlin's disintegration thesis, it appears that the thesis itself does not amount to a rejection of Mill's view. The crucial issue which divides Devlin from Mill's supporters turns on the apparently false factual claims with which Devlin tries to back up his thesis.

II. MILL'S STABLE SOCIETY

But it may now be suggested that Devlin's arguments help to focus on the limitations of Mill's individualism.[18] The sources of harm are numerous, and Mill's individualism made him very sensitive to harm caused by one individual to another. But, on the other hand, it also led him to ignore the cohesive effects of having shared values and institutions. Mill therefore failed to appreciate a very important source of harm — the harm to society caused by the undermining of these institutions and the violation of the shared values. Although such harm can be assimilated into his concept, he tended to ignore it and concentrate on harm to assignable individuals.

This criticism of Mill is unjustified. In a passage in his essay on Coleridge, Mill himself stresses the importance of shared values in maintaining a stable society. This essay was written for Radicals and Liberals,[19] and so he underlined, and perhaps even overemphasized, those aspects of Coleridge's view from which he believed that they had most to learn. However, although he made some amendments to the passage when he reprinted the essay later on in *Dissertations and Discussions*, he never gave up its crucial points, and the passage is reproduced in successive editions of his *A System of Logic*.[20] The context of his discussion is his attack on the radicalism of the eighteenth-century French thinkers. He argues that in their attempt to wipe out old beliefs, institutions, and practices which they found defective, they overlooked the cohesive effects and the sense of unity which these institutions and practices generated. They destroyed without replacement, and thereby subverted not merely what was bad in society, but also the very conditions of a stable society. Mill mentioned three such conditions.

First, there is to be a system of education which disciplines and restrains people from giving vent to their selfish and anti-social impulses.

Next, there must be a feeling of allegiance or loyalty to something or other — to a common God or gods, to certain persons, to laws, ancient liberties and ordinances, and, Mill later adds, to 'the principles of individual freedom and political and social equality, as realized in institutions which as yet exist nowhere, or exist only in a rudimentary state'.[21]

Finally, it is important to have a feeling of common interest among those who live in the same society. Here Mill has in mind the feeling of nationality, though not, as he says, in its 'vulgar sense' where it is identified with hostility to foreigners, and foreign ideas and institutions. In *Representative Government* he writes:

This feeling of nationality may have been generated by various causes. Sometimes it is the effect of identity of race and descent. Community of language, and community of religion, greatly contribute to it. Geographical limits are one of its causes. But the strongest of all is identity of political antecedents; the possession of a national history, and consequent community of recollections; collective pride and humiliation, pleasure and regret, connected with the same incidents in the past. None of these circumstances, however, are either indispensable, or necessarily sufficient by themselves.[22]

But it is Mill's second condition which is most relevant to our immediate concerns. Mill evidently believes that *some* shared values are necessary to the stability of society. There must be

something which is settled, something permanent, and not to be called in question; something which, by general agreement, has a right to be where it is, and to be secure against disturbance, whatever else may change. . . . But in all political societies which have a durable existence, there has been some fixed point; something which men agreed in holding sacred; which, wherever freedom of discussion was a recognized principle, it was of course lawful to contest in theory, but which no one could either fear or hope to see shaken in practice; which, in short (except perhaps during some temporary crisis), was in the common estimation placed beyond discussion.[23]

These shared values would presumably embrace what Hart calls 'universal values', which are incorporated, at least to some degree, in the common morality of *all* societies.[24] They include the safety of life and the protection of persons from deliberately inflicted harm. But obviously Mill has in mind something more than the universal values. In referring to the necessity of loyalty to common gods, to laws, ancient liberties, and ordinances, he acknowledges the importance to particular societies of specific institutions and practices which are of no use to other societies. He adds that what enables a society to weather the storms caused by the collisions between different interests and groups is that the conflict does not affect the fundamental basis of the social union. [25]

In interpreting Mill's remarks, it should be noted that the three conditions he lays down for a stable society are not intended to be the criteria of a good society. A good society must of course be stable, and a stable society will satisfy these conditions. But not all stable societies are good. The feeling of loyalty may therefore attach itself to undesirable objects, such as outdated customs and practices. Mill is not committed to maintaining that the particular objects of this feeling should never change. His many remarks in the essays on Bentham and Coleridge on the reform of existing institutions and practices give a clear indication that it is not change as such, not even radical change, which he opposes. Thus, commenting on the Reform Bill of 1832, he states: 'The good it has done, which is considerable, consists chiefly in this, that being so great a change, it has weakened the superstitious feeling against great changes.'[26] Nor, it appears, does he seek to exclude the questioning of any particular belief which is essential to the stability of society. 'A person', he says,

accustomed to submit his fundamental tenets to the test of reason, will be more open to the dictates of reason on every other point. Not from him shall we have to apprehend the owl-like dread of light, the drudge-like aversion to change, which were the characteristics of the old unreasoning race of bigots.[27]

Who then is Mill's opposition? Surely 'the negative, or destructive philosophers; those who can perceive what is false, but not what it true; who awaken the human mind to inconsistencies and absurdities of time-sanctioned opinions and institutions, but substitute nothing in the place of what they take away';[28] those who 'threw away the shell without preserving the kernel; and attempting to new-model society without the binding forces which hold society together, met with such success as might have been anticipated'.[29]

The foundations of a particular society may be undesirable, but they should not be destroyed without first of all laying new foundations of common loyalty. All that a society holds sacred may be questioned, but not all should be questioned at the same time. At any particular moment there will be something settled, but what is settled is not necessarily the same from one moment to another.

Mill is concerned with promoting social reforms within a stable framework which preserves whatever residual value existing institutions and practices may have. In *Representative Government* he says that 'when Order and Permanence are taken in their widest sense, for the stability of existing advantages, the requisites of Progress are but the requisites of Order in a greater degree; those of Permanence merely those of Progress in a somewhat smaller measure.'[30] In the essay on Coleridge he uses 'permanence' in this same sense of stability. He wants to promote both 'permanence' and progress. And it is social stability through change that he stresses, and not the absence of change as such, even in fundamental institutions and practices.

For Mill, a good society must rise above the requirements of a stable society. The presence of a high degree of individual freedom is one of the conditions of a good society. Of course it is possible that respect for individual liberty can itself become an object of common loyalty, and thereby a source of social stability. Indeed, as we shall soon see, this possibility is envisaged by Mill. But at the moment it is important to note that although all societies need a degree of stability in order to survive, it does not follow that the greater the degree of stability, the better is the society. So suppose that it is true, as it has sometimes been alleged, that the cost of having a large measure of individual liberty is a degree of instability in social life, for allowing Millian 'experiments in living' may introduce an element of uncertainty into social life. We cannot be sure how individuals will exercise their freedom, what new styles of life will arise, and what values will be accepted or rejected. But for Mill this would be a small price to pay for the far greater benefits of freedom. Certainly such 'instability' is compatible with the existence of the necessary degree of regularity and security in social life, and is a very far cry from the chaos and social dissolution that Devlin's disintegration thesis conjures up.

Various versions of the idea, similar to Mill's, that some shared values, over and above the universal values common to all societies, are necessary for the continued existence and stability of society, have been expounded in the writings of sociologists and political scientists. The notion of a consensus is used to express this point of view.[31] It is interesting to note that on some accounts, shared values are necessary at a rather general level, and not with respect to specific issues like the importance of monogamy and Christian sexual morality that Devlin has in mind when he propounded his disintegration thesis. Thus some consensus theorists argue for the necessity of agreement about the basic constitutional rules of the society, and the values which are embedded in them.[32] These rules and values will of course vary from society to society. In complex societies one may not be able to find widespread agreement on anything so specific as particular moral codes regulating areas of conduct like sexual activity.

In *The Division of Labour*, Durkheim stresses the decreasing importance of 'mechanical solidarity' as opposed to 'organic solidarity' in providing the basis of social cohesion in modern societies. By the former he refers to the solidarity which arises out of the resemblances between members of a society, out of their common beliefs and sentiments. Durkheim calls the set of common values and beliefs the 'conscience collective'. The 'conscience collective' is the source of social cohesion in traditional societies. However, as societies get more complex, the extent to which beliefs and values are held in common diminishes, and mechanical solidarity is gradually replaced by organic solidarity, a solidarity based on the differences between men. The growth of division of labour results in the interdependence of individuals who pursue different occupations. This interdependence is the source of organic solidarity. But even in modern societies, mechanical solidarity has a residual role although the content of the 'conscience collective' changes drastically from that in traditional societies where it is religious in character.[33] In an essay, 'Individualism and the Intellectuals' published a few years after *The Division of Labour*, Durkheim argues that the values of individualism form the 'only system of beliefs which can ensure the moral unity of the country'.[34] Individualism recognizes the sacredness of the human person, and stresses the importance of safeguarding his rights and freedom. The weakening of individualism will lead to social dissolution, and hence the defence of the rights of the individual is also a defence of society's vital interests.

Durkheim's view, that in modern societies the only mechanical solidarity possible is that built on the values of individualism, closely resembles Mill's later account of the conditions of social stability. In amendments to his discussion of these conditions, Mill writes that the feeling of allegiance or loyalty may attach itself to 'the principles of individual freedom and political and social equality', and he believes that 'this is the only shape in which the feeling is likely to exist hereafter.'[35] So we see Mill both acknowledging the importance of shared values in promoting social stability, and at the same time committing himself to a belief in the fundamental value of individual freedom and of political and social equality.

Mill's emphasis on individual freedom also draws attention to the gap between maintaining, on the one hand, that certain shared values are necessary for social stability, and claiming on the other hand that these shared values may be imposed by legal coercion. For it is possible that at least in some cases, an enforced consensus will not produce the desired stability, and only the voluntary acceptance of shared values will do so. This seems to be Mill's view when he speaks of the general *agreement* in treating something as settled and not to be called in question.[36]

Finally, Mill's account of nationality reflects his belief that it is not just shared values which contribute towards social stability, but also many other factors like shared experiences, a common history, a common language, and identity of race. None of these, as he points out, is either indispensable or necessarily sufficient in ensuring stability, but each is often important. These factors may of course generate shared values, though not necessarily moral values. Similarities of tastes in food, dress, music, sport, forms of entertainment, and an enjoyment of, or participation in, ceremonies and rituals often draw people together. In looking for the sources of social stability, it is as much a mistake to ignore these factors as it is to exaggerate them. In any case it is certainly a mistake to assume that there is necessarily one set of values or factors which bind *all* the people in the society together. It is in this context that individual liberty acquires a special importance. It allows individuals to develop different interests, and to form or to join groups catering to these interests.

Groups with common interests are not necessarily formed consciously and deliberately, nor are they always deliberately sought after. An individual is born into a group, and the process of growing up in a society exposes him to a variety of interests. But without the freedom to move in and out of certain groups, the individual will feel stifled and unable to develop some of his interests, or to dissociate himself from interests he no longer shares, or demands and pressures that have become oppressive. The mere process of living in a society generates many bonds of social union, even when there is no one set of values or interests which all or most people in that society share. Differences and conflicts between groups need not loosen these bonds except when these differences range over a very wide area, and different groups cease to have some important overlapping interests. For example, if the main groups in society are divided along racial, religious, cultural, and economic lines in such a manner that those of the same race also share the same religious and economic interests, then the mutual reinforcement of these powerful interests may be such as completely to overshadow all other interests. It is in this type of situation that conflicts between the main groups may have severely disruptive effects. On the other hand, in many societies, the absence of a shared sexual morality will in itself be no more disruptive than the absence of a fondness for the same type of food.

III. THE CONSERVATIVE THESIS

I shall now turn to the conservative thesis. In so far as this is supposed to provide an alternative justification of the legal enforcement of the shared morality, it must not fall back on the claim that such enforcement is needed to prevent society from collapse or disintegration. Devlin himself does not distinguish between the disintegration and the conservative thesis. But in his book, *Law, Morality and Religion in a Secular Society*, Basil Mitchell tries to clarify and develop some of Devlin's arguments.[37] He maintains that Devlin need not accept the two alternatives of either supporting his disintegration thesis with empirical evidence, or of turning it into the quite uninteresting thesis of identifying a society with a specific shared morality such that if there is any change in this morality, then the society has by definition 'disinte-grated'.[38] According to Mitchell, Devlin believes that the law has a right to protect the essential institutions of a society and the morality associated with these institutions.[39] The 'essential institutions' are not institutions without which society would disintegrate or weaken, nor are they institutions without which society would simply be different. A society would be different in some *fundamental* way in the absence of an essential institution. But what counts as a fundamental change in society? How do we distinguish between essential and non-essential institutions?

In illustrating the idea of an essential institution, Mitchell refers to the Franks Report on Oxford University, and here he provides one criterion of what an essential institution is. 'College life' and the tutorial system are regarded by the report as centrally important because, though other univer-sities have their own virtue, 'the distinctive merits of Oxford are bound up with *these* institutions.'[40] From this, and another illustration which Mitchell gives later, namely, the preservation of the Welsh language and the Welsh Sunday because they are 'characteristically Welsh',[41] it is clear that for him an institution is essential to a society if it is characteristic or distinctive of that society. But it is not at all obvious that the law is justified is protecting the essential institutions in this sense. Mitchell gives no sustained or clear arguments here. He seems to appeal to the value of diversity among societies, and describes this as 'a simple extension to nations and other cultural groups of the principle to which Mill attached so much importance in relation to individuals, "there is no reason that all human existence should be constructed on some one or some small number of pat-terns." '[42] But Mill's principle is meant to promote individual liberty against the dominant pressures of a society. When an apparently similar principle is applied to societies instead of individuals, it is not a 'simple extension' of Mill's principle, but an entirely different principle which may well threaten that very individual liberty that he tried so hard to defend. A totalitarian nation, free from external domination, can preserve its characteristic qualities by suppressing more and more of the freedom of its citizens, and in the name of nationalism individuals can be thrown into gaol. Mitchell speaks of the apparent indifference to the quality of the essential institutions of a society as a defect in Devlin's position. But his own position displays a similar defect. He is aware of this when he refers to 'the *Herrenvolk* doctrine of Nazi Germany or South African apartheid', but dismisses these as 'grave corruptions' of his principle.[43] However, if Nazis and South African whites had dispensed with false theories of racial superiority, and rested their cases simply on the need to maintain the distinctive essential institutions of their respective societies, then they would merely have invoked the very principle Mitchell is defending.

Mitchell's use of his principle is based on a confusion between the application of the principle to ward off external aggression by another society seeking to impose a different pattern of life on the unwilling members of a particular society, and its use to prevent an internal change in the established institutions of a society by its own members. When used against external aggression, his argument is the familiar one that nations have the right of self-determination. Those opposed to colonialism will find the argument most attractive, even when the external aggressor is a nation which is, by generally recognized standards, more advanced culturally, economically, and technologically. The argument is also powerful when it is used to support the rights of distinct and well-defined minority cultural groups to preserve their cultural life from the demands made by a different and dominating majority group within the same society. But the argument, thus restricted, is used defensively to protect a culturally distinct group of people from losing its identity as a result of external domination. On the other hand, Mitchell's 'extension' of Mill's principle seeks to justify the legal enforcement of the shared morality, and involves the imposition of a uniform pattern of conduct on all the members of a society. It is therefore paradoxical for him to claim that he is appealing to the value of diversity.

However, there are times when it appears that Mitchell's justification of the right of society to preserve its essential institutions and the associated morality leads to the protection of something other than society's currently shared morality. For essential institutions are those institutions which are peculiar to a particular society: the '*Welshness* of Wales', that which distinguishes Wales from England. But in this sense, what are most 'essential' to a particular society are not necessarily institutions and patterns of life which are now widely cherished, for societies may have become, with respect to these, 'largely indistinguishable' from one another. What marks out a particular society from others may be a way of life that once was but now largely is no more, except perhaps in the memories of a few of its nostalgic older members. In such a situation, Mitchell's argument would lend support to the restoration of a morality and way of life that was once widely shared, even though they may now be equally widely rejected.

There is therefore some ambiguity in Mitchell's position. On the one hand, he uses the notion of the characteristic or distinctive institutions of society to support Devlin's case for the legal enforcement of the shared morality, and he is then putting forward a version of the conservative thesis. But, on the other hand, his use of the notion of essential institutions sometimes seems to justify the enforcement of a pattern of conduct which is fast fading away, but which was most distinctive of that particular society. This latter thesis is not the conservative thesis, and is far removed from anything which Devlin himself wishes to maintain.

Devlin's conservative thesis is very much tied up with his frequent appeals to the feelings of intolerance, indignation, and disgust of the ordinary person. The lawmaker's duty is to preserve the essential institutions of his society. He does not have to ascertain whether the moral values embodied in these institutions are correct. His business is to find out what the shared morality is, and this can be done by ascertaining what is, and what is not, acceptable to the ordinary person. Devlin seems to imply that if the ordinary man feels strongly that a particular institution is important, then this is an essential institution which the law may seek to preserve. He justifies this by appealing to the democratic process. He claims that, as a matter of fact, issues of great moment are settled by the ordinary citizen. This is as it should be because in a democracy 'in the end the will of the people must prevail.'[44] To reject the views of the ordinary citizen as the final arbiter of how the law should act, and to appeal instead to the opinions of the educated élite in society, is undesirable. First, educated men often do not agree with one another on moral issues. Second, even if there is a consensus of moral opinions among the educated élite, to act on such a consensus is to set up an offensive intellectual oligarchy which is undemocratic in character.

Devlin's theory of democracy implies that it is undemocratic for legislators to enact unpopular laws. But if the criterion of whether a government is democratic is the extent to which it satisfies the will of the majority of the people, then dictatorships with mass support, but no free elections, would be quite 'democratic'. However, Devlin does not consistently hold on to his theory of democracy. He says that sometimes an ardent minority may carry greater weight than an apathetic majority,[45] and that a legislator's task is not just that of counting heads.[46] On these occasions, he seems to be moving toward the view that the opinions of the majority do not necessarily determine the acts of lawmakers, nor should they do so. Of course the views of the majority may sometimes set limits to what legislators may or may not be able to do, but legislators in a democracy are not obliged to follow these views, even when they are strongly and firmly held.

Neither Devlin nor Mitchell presents his conservative thesis as such for long. They often shift from the conservative to the disintegration thesis. But on those occasions when they do put forward the conservative thesis in its pure form, they seem to invoke either a mistaken theory of democracy, or that 'romantic conception of nationality' which Mitchell so rightly deplores in others.

IV. OFFENSIVE NUISANCES

Another criterion of an essential institution employed by Mitchell is that it is an institution with ramifications.[47] It is in this sense that marriage is an essential institution because of its connections with the institutions of parenthood and property. The ramifications of an institution obviously determine to some extent its importance in social life. But it is necessary to consider the different reasons for this since not all of them are relevant to the conservative thesis.

Mitchell refers to the difficulty of predicting the effects of social changes,[48] and it is true that the greater the ramifications of an institution, the more difficult it is to predict the likely consequences of a change in the institution. The legal protection of an essential institution may then be urged because of the fear that great harm would follow in the wake of the destruction or radical reform of the institution. But whatever the merits of this justification, neither Mitchell's nor Devlin's conservative thesis can rest simply on it, for they would then be falling back on the disintegration thesis, or on the generally accepted principle that the law may protect individuals from being harmed.

For there to be a distinct conservative thesis, society's right to preserve its essential institutions must then depend on other considerations. Perhaps it may be argued that the greater the ramifications of the institution, the greater will be the change in social life effected by the destruction or radical reform of the institution, and hence the greater the disturbance caused to individuals used to a particular social environment. When an essential institution, which is cherished in this way, is associated with a deeply felt and widely shared morality, public deviations from that morality may cause considerable offence to individuals. It may then be urged that it is unfair to deny a person a voice in determining what the social environment which he shares with others should be if he cannot, except with great difficulty, escape from that environment. Where there is a sufficiently strong chorus of voices against a particular sort of conduct, the law may legitimately seek to prohibit such public offensive acts.

If such acts may be prohibited, it is not simply because they are offensive, but because they are offensive nuisances. What converts an act which is merely offensive into one that is an offensive nuisance? One relevant factor is that the offensive conduct is 'thrust upon unwilling eyewitnesses'.[49] This requirement will not be satisfied simply because an act is committed in a public place in the sense in which a public place is any place that 'members of the public' are allowed to go, as opposed to a private house or garden. The act must be 'public' in a different sense, namely, that it is performed

in a place that people actually frequent and it is difficult for
them to avoid. A secluded beach, which the public are allowed
to use, but which as a matter of fact they do not visit, or can
very easily avoid using, is not a public place in the required
sense. So, for example, sexual intercourse performed on such
a beach, especially at an unearthly hour, is not an offensive
nuisance, even though the knowledge of it may strongly
offend many in society. On the other hand, if sexual intercourse takes place at peak hour in a busy shopping centre,
then it is obviously an offensive nuisance. Similarly, an
obscene film, discreetly advertised, and shown in a hall to
all adults who wish to see it, is not thrust upon an unwilling
audience. But the same film, shown in an open-air theatre,
visible to all passers-by, is an offensive nuisance.

It is not easy to spell out all the relevant considerations
which identify an act as an offensive nuisance, or which
justify legal intervention in such conduct. In his important
contribution, Joel Feinberg specifies two principles which
must be satisfied before offensive conduct may be legally
suppressed.[50] The first is that the conduct would offend
'almost any person chosen at random, taking the nation as
a whole'.[51] But he immediately restricts the scope of this
principle so that it does not apply to cases where the offence
is caused by the flaunting of abusive or insulting behaviour.
In these cases those who are offended may only be a racial
or religious minority, and the rest of society may be indifferent, and yet Feinberg believes that legal intervention is
justified. Why should this exception be made? Feinberg's
reply brings him close to a different principle, that offensive
conduct may be prohibited if it gives rise to the likelihood of
a breach of the peace. But in the end he veers away from this,
and argues that the law cannot permit those who are insulted
by offensive remarks to vent their anger in aggressive behaviour, but at the same time it is 'burdensome' for them to
live with their rage. Taken on its own, Feiberg's comment
here allows too much intervention because members of a
political party are often angered by the insults directed at the
party and its policies, and may well also find it 'burdensome'
to live with their anger. But Feinberg introduces a second
principle that the offensive conduct should not be prohibited

if those who are offended can avoid being offended without unreasonable effort or inconvenience. This is similar to the criterion we have just discussed.

For the purpose of *identifying* an act as an offensive nuisance, it seems enough to stick with our earlier criterion that it is an offensive act which is committed in a place frequented by those who are offended, and not easily avoidable by them. This applies to acts which are witnessed. Offensive smells and sounds require a slightly different treatment, since the source of the offence may be in private homes, and not necessarily in places frequented by the general public. But sounds and smells travel from one's private place to those of others and to public places. The principle which provides the basis for legal intervention in offensive nuisances is the same in all these cases. It is a principle of fairness. People who live together in a society have to share at least part of their environment with others with whom they may have little else in common. What happens in and around the places where people live, work, shop, eat, entertain or are entertained, is of common concern so long as it is clearly visible, audible, or within smelling distance. To avoid such places involves a sacrifice of a person's daily and perfectly legitimate activities. Fairness demands that everyone should have a say in what the common environment should be, and the problem is to decide how people's conflicting demands are to be settled. But there is no reason why people with totally different outlooks and tastes must share a totally common environment. Thus where some wish to swim in the nude whereas others are offended by the sight of naked bodies, the simple solution is to have separate beaches catering for each group. Non-harmful acts committed out of sight and out of hearing and smelling distance of others are done in non-public space, and there is no reason why others should have a say in what goes on. Since there is no common environment here, the argument from fairness does not apply.

The identification of an act as an offensive nuisance does not automatically justify the legal prohibition of the act. Its being an offensive nuisance in the required sense merely establishes a prima-facie case for legal intervention. But whether intervention is actually justified depends on the balancing of different considerations, and the claims of different groups. No doubt in many cases considerable weight has to be given to the preferences of the majority, but these preferences should not be allowed to override basic requirements of fairness and morality. A majority of whites who believe that it is all right for white couples to hold hands or kiss in public, but not for mixed couples to engage in similar acts, make a morally unacceptable distinction. The depth of the majority's offence need not be doubted. But there is no defensible principle of fairness or of morality which will support such discrimination. A law which discriminates in this way is as unjustified as one which prescribes a heavier penalty for a black man who rapes a white woman than for a white man who rapes a black woman.

Mill discusses offensive nuisances in one brief, and not very satisfactory, paragraph in *On Liberty*:

Again, there are many acts which, being directly injurious only to the agents themselves, ought not to be legally interdicted, but which, if done publicly, are a violation of good manners, and coming thus within the category of offences against others, may rightly be prohibited. Of this kind are offences against decency; on which it is unnecessary to dwell, the rather as they are only indirectly connected with our subject, the objection to publicity being equally strong in the case of many actions not in themselves condemnable, nor supposed to be so. (p. 153.)

He quite rightly points out that it is publicity of the act which is crucial, and that this class of acts includes both those which, when committed in private, are morally wrong, and those which are not. But he is too quick to place them 'within the category of offences against others' in virtue of their being violations of good manners. For an important issue is whether 'violations of good manners' can be considered a type of harm to others. According to the concept of harm Mill employs, and which I have discussed in Chapter 4, mere offence to others does not constitute harm to them. Public offensive acts do not harm others any more than private acts, although offence to feelings may be generally greater when acts are done in public than when they are committed in private. Mill gives the impression that these public acts are harmful to others because he is inclined to regard all justifiable intervention in conduct as being based on the prevention of harm to others. But what lifts these acts into the category of acts which may be interfered with is not the mere fact that they are offensive to others, but the different fact that they are offensive nuisances in the required sense. So here we have a class of conduct which both does not harm others, and which at the same time falls within the legitimate scope of legal intervention.

V. RELIGIOUS TOLERATION AND MORAL TOLERATION

Devlin also attempts to rebut Mill's case for the extension of toleration from the religious sphere to other areas of conduct. He distinguishes between religious toleration and the toleration of those who violate the shared morality of society by claiming that religious toleration is practicable because each person regards the religion of others as a lesser good rather than as evil.[52] But this fails to capture the depth of some religious differences. In any case, religious toleration also includes the toleration of atheists and agnostics, and the disagreements between some believers and militant atheists are much more profound that Devlin's account suggests. Devlin's argument carries the dangerous implication that religious toleration is not feasible or acceptable if we regard others' religion as evil.

To drive the wedge between religious toleration and what he calls 'moral toleration', Devlin also argues that we allow the law to punish the corruption of youth and public acts of indecency, whereas the religious conversion of a youth is allowed, and we do not try to suppress public religious ceremonies on the ground that they are offensive.[53] But Devlin misunderstands the rationale of prohibitions on offensive nuisances. Public acts of indecency are only one type of offensive nuisances, and acts which do not violate the shared morality of society can also be regarded as offensive nuisances. We try to regulate the time and place for the performance of certain acts. Even religious ceremonies can become offensive nuisances if they are conducted at inappropriate times and places. A noisy religious ceremony at a time when most people are asleep may be stopped, independently of whether we think the religion is true or false, good or bad.

It is odd that Devlin should respond to Mill's case for the extension of toleration by bringing in the offence of corrupting youth. The treatment of children falls outside the area of toleration demanded by Mill's liberty principle. Mill argues that we are not entitled to interfere with the conduct of normal adults simply because we disapprove of it. But the treatment of children falls under the legitimate scope of intervention. So both in the area of religion and sex, the law may properly interfere with the conduct of adults towards children. But whether it should actually interfere in each case depends on balancing a number of considerations, with the interest of the children being the most important factor. It does seem to be the case that greater latitude is given to parents in the religious instruction of their children than in their sexual instruction. But this is not because we think that parents should have absolute freedom over their children in religious matters. The decision of a Christian Scientist not to allow a blood transfusion to be given to his dying child may be overridden, even though a similar decision in the case of the adult himself should be respected. But religion often plays such a pervasive role in the lives of religious people that to refuse parents the right to convert their own children is to exclude children from participation in many activities. This removes one source of a happy family life organized round common activities and interests. But it may be that parents have been given too much liberty in religious matters. If it were practicable, it would be desirable to prevent parents from indoctrinating their children.[54]

7

Paternalism

I. WEAK PATERNALISM

Mill's rejection of paternalism forms part of his liberty principle, but it is such an important part that he explicitly spells out his anti-paternalism immediately after stating that the prevention of harm to others is the only legitimate basis of interference with the freedom of individuals.

His own good, either physical or moral, is not a sufficient warrant. He cannot rightfully be compelled to do or forbear because it will be better for him to do so, because it will make him happier, because, in the opinions of others, to do so would be wise, or even right. (p. 73.)

But Mill's anti-paternalism does not extend to 'children and persons under age'.[1] He also allows us forcibly to prevent a person from crossing an unsafe bridge.[2] But here he assumes that the person is unaware of the dangerous condition of the bridge, and that he does not wish to fall into the river. It is his ignorance which justifies a temporary restriction of his freedom. Interference is justified only if there is not time to warn the person about the danger. Mill generalizes by claiming that interference is unjustified unless the person is 'a child, or delirious, or in some state of excitement or absorption incompatible with the full use of his reflecting faculty' (p. 152).

In trying to understand the nature and scope of Mill's anti-paternalism, it is useful to bear in mind two different aspects of a person's conduct: the decision-aspect and the consequence-aspect. The former refers to the different ways in which an agent's decision to act in a particular manner is vitiated or impaired, or his consent to certain acts is not 'full and free'. Thus a person may commit a dangerous act without realizing, or fully appreciating, its danger. This is the case with the person crossing the unsafe bridge. On the other hand, the consequence-aspect refers to the undesirable consequences of a person's act, as for example the fact that the act will harm him or produce other undesired effects.

109

The cases which Mill excludes from the scope of his anti-paternalism are cases in which both the decision- and the consequence-aspects are present. Thus when Mill refers to children, it is evident that he believes that they lack certain capacities that normal adults have. Children, especially very young children, have not developed sufficiently their emotional and intellectual capacities, and they also lack the degree of knowledge and experience needed for meaningful choices.

An analysis of Mill's arguments and examples will show that he is opposed to strong paternalism but that he favours a degree of weak paternalism.[3] Strong paternalism maintains that we are justified in interfering to prevent a person from harming himself even when his decision is fully voluntary or totally unimpaired. Weak paternalism is the doctrine that we are justified in interfering to prevent a person from harming himself only when there is a defect in his decision to engage in the self-harming activity. Weak paternalism therefore justifies intervention when both the decision- and consequence-aspects are present, whereas strong paternalism justifies intervention by reference to the consequence-aspect alone.

An agent's decision to perform a particular act may be affected by a variety of factors which reduces the significance to be attached to the decision. A brief discussion of some of these factors will help in the understanding of weak paternalism.

First, a person may lack some relevant knowledge. This can take several forms. An agent may do something without being aware of the harmful consequences of his acts, and there may be reason to believe that had he known these consequences, he would not have acted in the way he did. An obvious case of this is the taking of a medicine with harmful side-effects unknown to the patient. But a person may also be lacking in knowledge not with respect to the consequences of his act, but to the nature of the act. An example of this would be a patient whose modesty is outraged by a doctor who pretends that he is giving her some special medical treatment. Lack of knowledge is often, as in this case, the result of fraudulent or misleading representation by others.

Secondly, there is lack of control. Sometimes a person may be aware of the consequences of his act, but because of temporary emotional unbalance, may be unable to appreciate the full significance of these consequences, and to exercise rational judgement with respect to them. Emotional unbalance may be caused by grief, distress, or severe strains. There is also another type of factor. Some drugs are severely addictive, and though the initial decision to take them is freely made, the subsequent 'choices' to continue taking them are impaired by the agent's addiction.

Thirdly, there is undue influence. This can be exerted in different ways, in some of which there will be disagreement about whether or not undue influence was really present. Coercion is an example of undue influence, but there are also the pressures of economic inducements, and sometimes of customs and traditions. A person who would not otherwise perform an act may do so because of economic inducements. This is common enough, and does not normally raise questions about undue influence. There was, however, an interesting case in which an air-hostess, guilty of a breach of regulations, consented to be caned by the manager of her company as an alternative to dismissal or being grounded, which would have meant the loss of her 'flying pay'. The manager administered six cuts on her buttocks with a light cane. He was convicted of assault in spite of receiving her written consent.[4] The occasions on which economic inducements may be regarded as impairing a person's decision depend on a number of factors like the degree of reluctance of the consenting victim, the relative bargaining positions of the parties, the relationship between the parties, and the nature of the available alternatives. No sharp line can be drawn between the situations in which undue influence is present and the situations in which it is not. The pressures exerted by customs and traditions are also sometimes of such great strength as to be treated by some as a kind of 'undue influence'. Thus Glanville Williams observes that the consent to duelling was often given with great unwillingness and solely out of fear of being called a coward. When duelling was legally prohibited, unwilling duellists had an honourable excuse for not fighting, and were thereby freed from 'the tyranny of custom'.[5]

Persons whose decisions are substantially impaired in one of the ways specified above are likely later on to regret their decisions to engage in harmful conduct. Interference will, in retrospect, be accepted and appreciated. But the subsequent consent of the subject is not a necessary condition for the justification of weak paternalism. Suppose, for example, that the person crossing the unsafe bridge condemns our interference. This does not make the interference wrong. What it does is to make any further or subsequent interference wrong. But the original interference is still justified so long as it was not known at the time that the subject would not consent.[6] Weak paternalism insists on always maintaining some contact with a person's own preferences and values. It promotes each person's own good as defined by that person himself. It is not a cloak for enforcing the values and preferences of the person interfering or society at large.

However, in some cases, because of the nature of the impairment, it is not possible to discover what a person's real preferences and values are. This is true of those special categories of persons — children, the mentally subnormal, and the mentally ill — who lack the capacities of normal adults. We may not know how particular persons would choose if they ceased to be children, or to be mentally ill, or if they were not mentally subnormal. There is here the danger that interference may be designed to shape and develop their values and preferences in line with those of the interfering party. The subject who is interfered with in this way will come to approve of the intervention.[7] In order to reduce the dangers of such manufactured consent, we need something like the Rawlsian device of choosing in a hypothetical state called the original position.[8] In Rawl's theory of justice, rational and mutually disinterested persons choose from behind 'a veil of ignorance' the principles which are to govern the basic institutions of their society. The veil of ignorance deprives them of knowledge of their particular talents and abilities, their class interests or social positions, their conceptions of the good or their particular moral and religious views, their psychological make-up, and the stage of development of their society. It does not, however, rob them of information about general psychological laws, and general truths about the world, or the nature of human societies, or human nature. Persons in the original position will allow some interference with their conduct if they turn out to be children, or adults who lack certain normal capacities.

In adopting the device of the original position for the limited purpose of helping to determine the scope of weak paternalistic intervention in the conduct of special categories of persons, we are not committed to Rawls's ambitious policy of deriving principles of justice from the original position.[9] There is a much greater likelihood of agreement about interference on weak paternalistic grounds than about the fundamental principles of justice. For example, there will be agreement about the need to interfere to prevent harm, and to protect and develop the capacities for choice between alternative patterns of conduct. But there will also be disagreement, and in particular about how children are to be treated as they grow older.

It is possible that the accumulation of evidence will show that children, except when they are very young, do not lack many of the relevant capacities of normal adults.[10] If this is correct, then paternalistic intervention in children's conduct will in many cases be unjustified. But even so, there seems to be one important qualification. If we think that relatively young children are capable of making informed choices about sexual matters, we should then be prepared to tolerate sexual relations between children of about the same age. But it does not follow that we should also tolerate the same type of sexual relations between a child and an adult. If we left children completely free to enter into any relationship with anybody they wish, they are likely to be exploited by some adults with much greater experience.

This brief discussion of paternalism is sufficient to show that Mill is quite consistent in accepting weak paternalism while at the same time rejecting the right of society to impose its value on individuals. There are at least three differences between the two doctrines.

1. Weak paternalism involves the protection of individuals from harming themselves in situations where their decisions are impaired. On the other hand, in order to enforce society's shared values the law may interfere even when a person's decision to engage in an activity is fully voluntary and clearly informed Thus to prevent freely consenting adult homosexuals

from indulging in homosexual activities in private simply because these activities violate the shared morality of society, is to enforce this morality, but the prohibition cannot be justified on weak paternalistic grounds.

2. Weak paternalism is not concerned to punish moral wickedness. Indeed paternalistic intervention only takes place when the agent's decision is impaired in some way, and from the moral point of view, this is generally regarded as reducing his moral culpability. A person who acts as a fully free moral agent in violating the accepted morality of society is outside the pale of paternalistic intervention, but, on the other hand, he is precisely the sort of person against whom society may wish to enforce its shared values.

3. The basis of paternalistic intervention is confined to an appeal to the interests of particular persons who are to be prevented from harming themselves. This is as true of strong paternalism as it is of weak paternalism. But the enforcement of society's shared values often relies on appeals to all sorts of more general considerations, including, as we have noticed, the protection of the distinctive institutions of society. Paternalism focuses attention constantly on the interests of the person with whom we are interfering. The enforcement of society's shared values is only too likely to sacrifice these interests to the often unreasoning and unreasonable anger and hatred of the community.

II. STRONG PATERNALISM

Whereas Mill is prepared, to some extent, to accept weak paternalism, he seems to be absolutely opposed to strong paternalism. One argument Mill uses against strong paternalism is often cited:

But neither one person, nor any number of persons, is warranted in saying to another human creature of ripe years, that he shall not do with his life for his own benefit what he chooses to do with it. He is the person most interested in his well-being: ... with respect to his own feelings and circumstances, the most ordinary man or woman has means of knowledge immeasurably surpassing those that can be possessed by any one else. The interference of society to overrule his judgement and purposes in what only regards himself must be grounded on general presumptions; which may be altogether wrong, and even if right, are as likely as not to be misapplied to individual cases, by persons no better acquainted with the circumstances of such cases than those are who look at them merely from without. (p. 133.)

Certainly Mill is here claiming that generally a person knows his own interests best. But it has often been argued that this is only a defeasible general presumption, and that elsewhere, in *Principles of Political Economy*, Mill himself recognized cases in which the government knows a person's interests better than the person himself. One such case is the provision of education. Mill argues: 'The uncultivated cannot be competent judges of cultivation. Those who most need to be made wiser and better, usually desire it least, and if they desired it, would be incapable of finding the way to it by their own lights.'[11] Mill is discussing the limits of the doctrine of *laissez-faire* in social and economic life generally. Government must step in to provide services that individuals will not be able to provide for themselves as effectively. But Mill does not argue that the government is justified in coercing normal adults to do certain things for their own good. His position is that the government should provide services which people are free to use if they so choose.

So Mill does not jump from the acknowledgement that individuals are sometimes not the best judges of their own interests to the advocacy of strong paternalism. He is convinced that coercive interference tends to stunt the person's capacities, and is at least to some extent degrading.

To be prevented from doing what one is inclined to, or from acting according to one's own judgment of what is desirable, is not only always irksome, but always tends, *pro tanto*, to starve the development of some portion of the bodily or mental faculties, either sensitive or active; and unless the conscience of the individual goes freely with the legal restraint, it partakes, either in a great or in a small degree, of the degradation of slavery.[12]

But when a government merely provides individuals with various facilities, and leaves them free to avail themselves of these facilities, it does not restrict their freedom. Mill therefore justifies non-coercive government activity.

It is of course part of the price of allowing individuals freedom to choose for themselves and to conduct experiments in living that they sometimes make mistakes and harm themselves. But it is not conducive to the development of individuals that they should be fenced in from all sorts of harm. However, it is plausible to argue that some self-harming actions should be treated differently. In order to develop oneself in any direction one must preserve a minimum of intellectual and physical powers and capacities. If, through his risky actions, an individual kills himself, or destroys these powers and capacities, then he removes the very prerequisites of his self-development. To prevent him from harming himself in these ways is to preserve opportunities for his future development, and to leave him with the ability to choose between different patterns of life. So, it may be argued, some cases of strong paternalism help rather than hinder the process of self-development.

To this Mill's reply is that a person may place such a high value on what he does that the risk of death or grave harm is worth taking: 'no one but the person himself can judge of the sufficiency of the motive which may prompt him to incur the risk.'[13] He should be warned of the danger and of the risk he is taking, but once he knows this but still persists in going ahead, he should be allowed to do so.

But it is sometimes said that, for example, compelling people to wear seat belts is only 'a trivial piece of compulsion' and that the risks of not wearing seat belts are disproportionate to the benefits. On the other hand, it is conceded that the risks involved in mountain climbing may be proportionate to the benefits it gives.[14] Mill's point is directed precisely against this type of argument. For many of those who drive without seat belts will disagree that their case is very different from that of the mountain climber. They will claim, with some justice, that they value not wearing seat belts much more than is made out. By rejecting their own assessment of their values we run the risk of evaluating the benefits of an activity by our own standards rather than by their standards. If people who are aware of the risks involved in not wearing seat belts still persist in not wearing them, it may be that they find wearing them a bigger nuisance and a greater hindrance to their enjoyment than we do, or because they attach less importance to the risk of harm relative to the satisfaction of their present wants. We admire those who climb dangerous mountains, or those who sail alone round the world, and because of this we think that the benefits they obtain are worth the risks they run. Similarly, when people defy their doctor's 'orders' and continue to work hard we understand and perhaps even approve of this if we appreciate the value of the work. But where we disapprove of an activity, or cannot appreciate it, we tend to think that the agent himself derives little benefit from it. In these ways the practice of strong paternalism easily becomes a cloak for the imposition of our values on those who are coerced. But if we do not allow paternalism to slide into the enforcement of our values on others, then we have no clear basis for distinguishing between activities we are prepared to permit and those we wish to suppress.

Moreover, the desire to seek danger is often the product of a certain type of personality and temperament that some people take pride in cultivating. To interfere with their risky conduct is to deny them the opportunity to pursue their own plans of life. Friends and relatives may sometimes interfere out of love and concern. But a person can break away from them, and even in the last analysis invoke the law to restrain them. But when the state itself interferes, then there is no escape.

III. SELLING ONESELF INTO SLAVERY

The consistency of Mill's rejection of strong paternalism is called into question when he refuses to allow a person voluntarily to sell himself into slavery. Mill's argument is worth quoting:

> By selling himself for a slave, he abdicates his liberty; he foregoes any future use of it beyond that single act. He therefore defeats, in his own case, the very purpose which is the justification of allowing him to dispose of himself. . . . The principle of freedom cannot require that he should be free not to be free. It is not freedom to be allowed to alienate his freedom. (p. 158.)

Mill's argument is unclear. He allows us to give up part of our freedom, as we constantly do when we enter into contracts. Nor is it the case that in any transaction that involves giving up some of our freedom, the freedom that we gain must be greater than the freedom that we lose. For freedom is not the only valuable end, and sometimes a net loss of freedom, voluntarily contracted, is more than made up by a gain in other benefits like income and material comforts. Mill has said nothing to indicate that he would prohibit such exchanges of freedom for other goods. Indeed in discussing the Mormon institution of polygamy, he explicitly argues against intervention even though the principle of liberty is violated: 'far from being coutenanced by the principle of liberty, it is a direct infraction of that principle, being a mere riveting of the chains of one half of the community, and an emancipation of the other from reciprocity of obligation towards them.' (p. 148.) Intervention is not justified because the marriage is voluntary since many women 'prefer being one of several wives to not being a wife at all'. So slavery is different, not because it involves a sacrifice of freedom, but because the freedom is given up completely and permanently.

We can imagine a situation in which a person has voluntarily sold himself into perpetual slavery. After a few years he greatly detests his condition and very much regrets having sold himself as a slave. His health suffers from the demanding work required of him, and he now refuses to obey the slave-holder any longer. The slave-holder invokes the law. Sanctions will be used to enforce the terms of the contract. The law thereby not merely permits, but also uses sanctions to support, the slave-holder's harming of the slave. Now this example seems to fall between cases of self-harming conduct and cases of conduct harmful to others. The example is not a clear case of the harm done by one person to another with his full consent. For in these cases when *A* harms *B*, *B* consents to the harm and does not withdraw his consent at the time the harm is inflicted. But perpetual slavery is also not a clear case of conduct which harms others in the sense which allows the state to interfere. In the clear cases, one person harms another who has at no time consented to be harmed.

It is possible that Mill wishes to treat at least some cases in which one person harms another in conformity with an earlier contractual agreement, but against the person's present wishes, as conduct causing harm to others against their will, and therefore as conduct coming within the legitimate scope of legal intervention. If this is the case, then interfering with such contracts is not a paternalistic act but one designed to prevent harm to others. Since the prevention of harm to others is not a sufficient condition for intervention one has to balance the advantages and disadvantages of interfering against those of not doing so. In the case of perpetual slavery, the harm done to a subsequently unwilling person is very grave, and there will be sufficient reason for not recognizing the slavery contract. But if there is a 'slavery' contract, renewable at frequent intervals, and imposing limits to what may be required of the slave without his existing consent, this should be enforceable.[15] For although the individual would still be giving up his freedom, the contract will not be radically different from other freedom-limiting contracts, and at regular intervals he has the option of ceasing to be a slave. It is also important to note that the argument I have suggested on Mill's behalf does not prohibit a person from voluntarily becoming a lifelong slave of another person. But it supports the refusal to give legal recognition to contracts for perpetual slavery.

IV. HARMING ONE'S LATER SELF

I have suggested that selling oneself into slavery can be brought under Mill's principle which justifies the prevention of harm to others. There is another line of argument which stretches the category of conduct which harms others without their consent even further, and I wish now to explain and resist this argument.

D. H. Regan claims that some acts which are normally regarded as self-harming can be treated as acts which harm another person.[16] What we ordinarily regard as different time-segments of the same person can more appropriately be viewed as different persons. Thus the motor-cyclist at the time of his choosing to ride without a helmet, and the motor-cyclist who later meets with a serious accident, are two different persons. If there are two different persons, then the act of riding without a helmet is really an act which harms another person, the motor-cyclist's later self. So intervention in the act comes within the scope of Mill's liberty principle. This account draws on Derek Parfit's work on personal identity.[17] Parfit refers to the criterion of psychological connectedness for distinguishing between persons. This considers the degree of similarity in the psychological characteristic at different times.

However, Regan seems to adopt a narrower criterion. He writes: 'the motor-cyclist is a different person, in the relevant respect, if he is no longer the sort of person who would ignore his future wellbeing for the sake of small increments of present utility.'[18] So if the motor-cyclist is likely, after being harmed in an accident, to regret the past act of riding without a helmet and to change his attitude towards risk, then there is a different person who has been harmed. But since a person's attitude towards risk is only one of his psychological characteristics, it is likely that a change here is not accompanied by a change in other psychological characteristics. This leads to a situation in which for some purposes the same person is present at two points in time, but for other purposes there are two different persons. Regan accepts this. He gives the example of someone who, at about the same time that he embezzles, also commits an unrelated act of aggravated assault. Suppose that after ten years he has grown more honest and would no longer embezzle. However, he has not changed in his attitude towards physical aggression. Regan thinks that it is inappropriate to punish him for embezzlement, but proper to punish him for assault. This situation can be handled easily enough by the resources we ordinarily use of saying that one and the same person is to be punished for assault but not for embezzlement. But if we adopt Regan's criterion of when we have the same person, we face the problem of determining the relation between the assailant and the person who is not punished for embezzlement. They are not the same person, but there is no way of punishing the assailant which does not also adversely affect the other person. If the assailant is imprisoned, the other person will also find himself in gaol. If the assailant is fined, then the resources of the other person are also reduced. All their desires, interests, and values are the same. Even Siamese twins are not so closely bound together.

Similarly, if we apply Regan's criterion of personal identity, we would have to say that the motor-cyclist, who rides without a helmet, is not the only person affected by punishment. An ordinary person has many projects, not all of which may fit into a single, over-all plan. For example, he has made promises which he intends to keep, and these promises are unrelated to his desire to ride without a helmet. By punishing him for riding without a helmet, the state may deprive him of the opportunity to keep some of his promises. Punishing the motor-cyclist will therefore also interfere with the freedom of an innocent person, the promise-maker. This seems unfair. So even if we accept Regan's view that the motor-cyclist's act can harm another person, the same reasoning also provides us with a basis for not punishing him, and it is not clear how we are to balance the case for punishing the guilty motor-cyclist against the claims of the innocent promise-maker.

Punishing the motor-cyclist is of course a preventive measure taken to reduce the harm caused if there is an accident. So the real offence of the motor-cyclist is that of engaging in a dangerous activity which is likely to cause harm to another person, namely, his later self. It is of course perfectly proper to prevent someone from performing a dangerous act even though not all such acts will actually cause harm to others. For example, not every single act of driving at high speed through a busy street will cause harm. It is enough that every such act is likely to cause harm. However, in the ordinary case of dangerous driving, although actual harm to others may not be inflicted, there are actual persons who are likely to he harmed, and who therefore need protection. But in the case of the motor-cyclist, if there is no accident, then it is not just the case that he does not harm another person. There will also be no other person to be harmed. The accident both gives birth to and harms the later self. But still, there are other analogies to draw on. It is certainly not the case that the only type of harm to others is harm to actual persons who already exist at the time of the relevant act. Environmental pollution may not harm the existing population, but it will harm future generations. No doubt in this case the people who will be harmed will come into existence independently of the harmful act, but it is unclear whether this is a significant difference.

But there is one important difference. Death is not a relevant harm in the case of the motor-cyclist. For if the accident causes death, then it does not produce a later self who is harmed. Death, at least instant death which leaves no time for regret, ensures that there is no birth of the later self, and so death makes the accident self-harming but not harmful to another person. This point is recognized by Terry S. Kogan who adopts Regan's position.[19] Kogan argues that the account of later selves cannot be used to justify state intervention in suicide.

In order for Mill's justification of state intervention to apply intertemporally, it is necessary that one make a reasonable prediction that future selves will disidentify with the present self. But where it is clear that there will be *no* future selves, such prediction becomes meaningless. Since there will be no future intertemporal 'others', suicide is a purely self-regarding action.[20]

But the same point applies to all risky actions which cause death, or severe brain damage in which the person, while still alive, is unconscious or is incapable of formulating new values and plans of life, and is therefore incapable of renouncing his old values and attitudes. From such a brain-damaged being no later self can emerge to be harmed. It is paradoxical that activities which are likely to cause these types of serious harm fall outside the scope of Regan's and Kogan's new defence of paternalism, whereas activities which are likely to cause lesser harm can be interfered with.

Kogan also claims that there is evidence to support the view that a person will reject his earlier goals as a result of the traumatic experience of a serious accident.[21] If this is true, then it presumably applies even when a helmet or seat belt was worn. The accident may, for example, be caused by driving at high speed, or by the failure to pay sufficient attention, and the person now regrets and rejects his previous attitudes. If it is the trauma of the serious accident which causes the change in him, sufficient for a later self to emerge, then this change can come about even when he had taken the precaution of wearing a helmet or seat belt. Now those who support the compulsory wearing of helmets and seat belts do not of course claim that the *rate* of accidents is thereby reduced. What is rightly claimed is that *when* there are accidents, the wearing of helmets and seat belts reduces the extent of harm caused. No doubt death and severe brain damage will be among the serious harm that will be reduced. But we recall that on Regan's and Kogan's account, if there is death or severe brain damage, then there is no harm to others as there are no later selves. This being the case, the probability that the wearing of seat belts and helmets reduces the incidence of these types of harm constitute a reason *against* requiring them to be worn. For when the harm caused is death or severe brain damage, the victim is the present self and not a later self. Accidents which result in these types of harm do not therefore cause harm to others, but are purely self-harming. If the wearing of seat belts and helmets reduces the number of deaths and cases of severe brain damage, then it increases the harm caused to others by reducing the number of self-harming actions. This is a surprising but inescapable implication of an appeal to the idea of harm to later selves.

8

Freedom of Expression

In defending freedom of expression, Mill assumes that it is
no longer necessary to restate its political function in protecting citizens from the operations of corrupt and tyrannical
governments. Instead he is particularly concerned to establish a case for the freedom to express unpopular views which
go against the prevailing public opinion. A person's right to
express his opinion does not depend on the extent to which
his view is shared by others. 'If all mankind minus one were
of one opinion, and only one person were of the contrary
opinion, mankind would be no more justified in silencing
that one person, than he, if he had the power, would be
justified in silencing mankind.' (p. 79.)

Superficially, Mill's arguments for freedom of expression
are simple enough. He himself summarizes them as follows:
'We can never be sure that the opinion we are endeavouring
to stifle is a false opinion; and if we were sure, stifling it
would be an evil still.' (p. 79.) But if one examines the way in
which these arguments are elaborated, one soon discovers
that Mill's summary of them is in fact oversimplified. One of
his central arguments is based on the notion of human
fallibility. But this argument is ambiguous, and depending on
how it is interpreted, it in fact establishes two very different
connections between human fallibility and the allowance of
freedom of expression, and corresponding to these two
connections, there are two different notions of the value of
the search for truth.

Sometimes Mill points to human fallibility as a reason for
not suppressing an opinion because we may be mistaken, and
in suppressing a purportedly false opinion, we may in fact be
suppressing what in future will be shown to be true. Thus he
points to the mistakes, arising out of human fallibility, which
led to the deaths of Socrates and Jesus and to the persecution
of the early Christians. Those who engage in mistaken acts of
suppression are often sincere men who believe in the rightness

of what they are doing. Indeed in the Roman emperor Marcus Aurelius we had a man who was intellectually and morally far superior to the average person. Yet if such a man could make mistakes, how much more likely are ordinary persons to do so. Sincerity and nobleness of purpose, intellectual and moral wisdom do not rule out the fallibility which is shared by all human beings. Even when our beliefs are generally and widely accepted by the rest of our society, and indeed by the whole age, this is no guarantee that we are not mistaken. We are not justified in accepting the optimism of Dr Johnson that persecution will not suppress the truth for ever, that the truth will always survive the ordeal of persecution, and has the intrinsic ability of ultimately triumphing over error. This is 'idle sentimentality': 'History teams with instances of truth put down by persecution.' (p. 89.) The absence of freedom of expression also creates an atmosphere in which men fear to pursue their opinions to unorthodox and socially unacceptable conclusions. Instead they will trim their beliefs to suit the existing orthodoxies, and in such an atmosphere of intellectual timidity and conformity, no new true beliefs will emerge to challenge prevailing views.

Let's call this the Avoidance of Mistake Argument. Its central claim is that human fallibility makes necessary freedom of expression if we are to avoid suppressing true beliefs. This first argument should be distinguished from what may be called the Assumption of Infallibility Argument.

The latter is put forward by Mill when he considers an objection to the Avoidance of Mistake Argument. According to this objection, from the fact that we may act mistakenly in suppressing a true opinion, it does not follow that we should not act at all. If we genuinely, and on good grounds, believe that an opinion is false and that its expression will have pernicious consequences, we should not be deterred from suppressing it by the mere possibility that our views may be mistaken. At this point Mill replies: 'Complete liberty of contradicting and disproving our opinion is the very condition which justifies us in assuming its truth for purposes of action: and on no other terms can a being with human faculties have any rational assurance of being right.' (p. 81.) The reply tries to undercut the claim that we could have good grounds for believing that our opinion is true in the absence of freedom of discussion. Unlike the earlier argument for freedom of expression which stresses the dangers of making mistakes, this new argument emphasizes the lack of rational assurance of fallible men in the truth of their beliefs. According to the Assumption of Infallibility Argument, the opinion we desire to suppress may very well be false, as we claim it to be, but, as fallible beings, we can have no rational assurance that it is false unless there is freedom to discuss it. In the absence of freedom of discussion we are not entitled to believe that it is false, even though it may in fact be false. To claim that we know it to be false is to make an implicit claim to our own infallibility. So unless there is freedom of expression fallible men can have no rational grounds for believing that their opinions are true. Mill is no longer referring to the benefits of holding true beliefs. He has now shifted his attention to the rationality of our beliefs, and freedom of expression is defended as an indispensable condition for the holding of rational beliefs.

The Assumption of Infallibility Argument is closely related to a third argument of Mill's that even if an opinion is false, it would be wrong to stifle it. Let's call this the Necessity of Error Argument. It maintains that in the absence of freedom of discussion one will not appreciate the full meaning of the opinion. The true belief will be held as a 'dead dogma'. By this Mill means that the person who holds such a belief will not be properly influenced by it. He will not appreciate to any considerable degree what he is committed to when he accepts the opinion. At the same time his acceptance of this belief will prevent him from accepting other beliefs that appear to oppose it, but may in fact be no more than complementary to it, or perhaps a refinement of it, or even completely unrelated to it. The absence of freedom of discussion also prevents us from knowing 'the grounds of the opinion'. Men will hold on to a belief quite independently of the balance of arguments and evidence for and against it. Their belief will therefore be held in a rigid and dogmatic way, and they are unable to adapt it to changing circumstances. If, for example, there are strong arguments limiting the area of application of a rule, they will not appreciate them. They will apply the rule

indiscriminately, overlooking what may well be proper exceptions to it. They may even insist on applying it in situations
which the rule was not meant to cover. Mill goes on to say
that the effort to know the grounds of an opinion cultivates
the intellect and judgement. On the other hand, the absence
of freedom of discussion leads to the atrophy of these faculties.

Once again it is not simply the having of true opinions that
Mill values. Rather, it is the way in which the truth is held.
He wants people to hold their opinions in a rational manner,
with a knowledge of the significance of these opinions and
the grounds for them, and with a willingness to change or
modify them in the light of new arguments and evidence.
Referring to those who hold a true opinion without knowing
the grounds of the opinion, he says that the true opinion
'abides as a prejudice, a belief independent of, and proof
against, argument' (p. 96). There is therefore for Mill a
distinction between having true opinions and what he calls
'knowing the truth'. Whereas the Avoidance of Mistake
Argument stresses the value of having true opinions, both the
Assumption of Infallibility and the Necessity of Error
Arguments emphasize the importance of trying to know the
truth.

The value of having true beliefs lies in the good consequences produced by the beliefs. True beliefs promote progress
and improve the welfare of men. But a man's views on
morality, politics, and religion are intimately linked to his
personality. The beliefs he has, and the way he holds them,
help to define the sort of person he is. The mere fact that he
has true beliefs is not enough. We do not think much of a
person who simply holds on to true beliefs but has no clear
understanding of them or of the reasons for holding them. In
assessing the type of person he is, or whether his life is worthy
of imitation, we will look at his personal qualities, and these
include the way he holds his views about what is and what is
not desirable, the influences these views have on his daily life
as displayed in the manner he applies them to particular
situations and the way he reacts to changing circumstances.
For Mill, it really is important not only what beliefs men
hold, but also what manner of men they are that hold them.

Now true beliefs may be acquired in all sorts of ways —

through revelation, indoctrination, manipulation of the sources of information and the media of communication, as well as through freedom of discussion. If a person's ultimate value is that all men should have true beliefs, no matter how these beliefs are generated, then he will cherish freedom of discussion only in so far as it promotes such true beliefs. Freedom of discussion then becomes simply a means to the promotion of true beliefs, and if it is not the most efficient and economical way of attaining this goal, there appears to be no reason why other means should not be adopted. In certain actual, and in many imaginable situations, it is, for example, possible that the cultivation of specific true beliefs in as many people as possible is best achieved through indoctrination. In these cases one who values freedom of discussion only as a means to the establishment and propagation of true beliefs will be prepared to ditch freedom. Mill in fact believes that true opinions are most likely to emerge through freedom of discussion. But some critics of his have pointed out that if he is wrong on this, he is committed to abandoning his liberal belief in freedom of discussion. Alternatively, it is maintained that it is only because Mill is sceptical about the truth of, for example, competing religious doctrines that he preaches religious toleration. All these objections overlook the importance that Mill attaches to trying to know the truth instead of merely having true opinions. Mill's critics tend to concentrate on his first argument for freedom of expression and to ignore his other arguments.[1]

Consider the case of religious toleration. One argument for it is the optimistic belief that though persecution can change men's outward behaviour, it cannot affect their views about what is true or false. Thus Locke argued that

Neither the profession of any articles of faith, nor the conformity to any outward form of worship . . . can be available to the salvation of souls unless the truth of one, and the acceptableness of the other unto God, be thoroughly believed by those that so profess and practice. But penalties are no way capable to produce such belief. It is only light and evidence that can work a change in men's opinions; which light can in no manner proceed from corporal sufferings or any other outward penalties.[2]

In a similar vein, Mill's disciple, John Morley, wrote:

Here is the radical fallacy of those who argue that people must use promises and threats in order to encourage opinions, thoughts, and feelings which they think good, and to prevent other which they think bad. Promises and threats can influence acts. Opinions and thoughts on morals, politics and the rest, after they have once grown in a man's mind, can no more be influenced by promises and threats than can my knowledge that snow is white or that ice is cold. You may impose penalties on me by statute for saying that snow is white, or acting as if I thought ice cold, and the penalties may affect my conduct. They will not, because they cannot, modify my beliefs in the matter by a single iota. One result of intolerance is to make hypocrites. On this, as on the rest of the grounds which vindicate the doctrine of liberty, a man who thought himself infallible either in particular or in general, from the Pope of Rome down to the editor of the daily newspaper, might still be inclined to abstain from any form of compulsion.[3]

But against this type of argument, even long before the awareness that modern techniques of propaganda and subtle manipulation of the social environment can radically change the beliefs of men, Pascal had already argued that the 'sickness' of religious disbelief can be cured if a man acted as if he believed in God. In the end he can work his way into genuine belief. (Whether genuine belief generated in this way will win him a place in Heaven, as Pascal thought, is more debatable, and I am inclined to think that a good God would, when confronted with such a man in the afterlife, tell him bluntly, 'Go to Hell.') I doubt that we can now be as confident as Locke was that only 'light and evidence' can change men's opinions, and consequently the argument from the ineffectiveness of persecution and intolerance in changing men's beliefs rests on dubious foundations.

Hence if freedom of discussion is supported solely by Mill's Avoidance of Mistake Argument, it will cut no ice with those who believe that they have the truth from some infallible source, and who further believe that it is easier for them to share the truth with others if freedom is not accorded to opposing false beliefs. Although he tries to forge a strong link between freedom of discussion and the true beliefs which in turn lead to the progress that men value, it is clear that as far as Mill himself is concerned, the ultimate defence of freedom of discussion lies elsewhere — in his Assumption of Infallibility and Necessity of Error Arguments. Though he thinks that in the end there would be a consensus of opinion on many currently contentious matters, he believes that this state of affairs is desirable only if it results from freedom of discussion. He does not regard peace and tranquillity, to which the absence of conflicting and contentious views gives rise, as intrinsically desirable, irrespective of how they were attained. In this he differs from so many of his critics who share the views of Fitzjames Stephen that if all men could be made, without too great cost, to have true opinions, this would be 'the greatest of all intellectual blessings'.[4] Whereas Stephen merely wanted men to have true beliefs, Mill wishes them to know the truth.

Mill admires rational and intellectually active men, and freedom of discussion is necessary for raising 'even persons of the most ordinary intellect to something of the dignity of thinking beings' (p. 95). For him thinking beings are those who seek to know the truth, and who are not afraid of pursuing a view to whatever conclusions it leads. They do not hold a view dogmatically. They adopt a certain attitude towards evidence and arguments which commits them to accept freedom of discussion so that all those who disagree with them will be allowed to state opposing views. A free atmosphere is necessary if there are to be thinking men, and thinking men would want freedom both for themselves and for others.

It is sometimes maintained that Mill cherishes freedom of discussion only for the élite. Certainly he recognizes that the intellectual powers and abilities of men differ greatly, and he believes that the intellectual élite of society has a special contribution to make. In an early essay he quotes with approval the remark, 'Some are wise, and some are otherwise',[5] and in the essay *On Liberty* he sees the élite as pioneers who will break through the barriers of custom to new and better ways of life. But freedom is not for them alone, and indeed he goes so far as to say explicitly that the chief benefit of freedom of discussion lies in what it can do for average human beings:

Not that it is solely, or chiefly, to form great thinkers, that freedom of thinking is required. On the contrary, it is as much and even more to enable average human beings to attain the mental stature which they are capable of. There have been, and may again, be, great individual thinkers in a general atmosphere of mental slavery. But there never has been, nor ever will be, in that atmosphere an intellectually active people. (p. 94.)

Mill, then, has a number of different arguments for freedom of expression. But he believes that these arguments are connected. Rational and thinking men, who seek to know the truth, are more likely to arrive at true opinions than those who wish to suppress false opinions. So, though in a particular case false opinions may prevail over true ones if freedom of discussion is permitted, in the long run many more true doctrines will be discovered in a free atmosphere, which breeds thinking men, than in an atmosphere where there are restrictions on freedom of expression.

Mill intends his powerful case for freedom of expression to apply to the important areas of 'morals, religion, politics, social relations, and the business of life' (p. 96). However, there are flaws in the details of his arguments.

He considers an objection to his Assumption of Infallibility Argument, that fallible beings cannot have a rational assurance that their opinions are true unless there is freedom of discussion. The objection tries to get round the Argument by avoiding the making of truth claims about an opinion. There are certain beliefs so useful to the well-being of society that it is the duty of government to protect these beliefs and to suppress the expression of opinions contrary to them. Such suppression would not, it is argued, be based on the assumption of infallibility since it rests on the claim that the belief is useful, and not on the claim that it is true. Mill makes two points against this objection. First, he says that the usefulness of an opinion is itself something about which men may dispute. We therefore can have no rational assurance that our view concerning the utility of an opinion is correct unless there is freedom of discussion, or unless we assume our own infallibility. Second, Mill maintains that no false belief is really useful, and so it is not possible to avoid making truth claims after all. To assess the usefulness of an opinion we have first to know whether or not the opinion is true.

Mill's first point does not in itself satisfactorily answer the objection. Consider the two statements p and q:

p = Members of race R are all incurably stupid.

q = The expression of statements about the stupidity of the members of any race will, in the present situation of racial tension and antagonism, lead to race riots.

In other words, q is a second-order statement about statements like p. Now if q is true, it provides a reason for suppressing the expression of p in certain contexts. Mill's point can be met so long as we remain free to dispute q. But q can be freely disputed even if p is suppressed. However, Mill's second point tries to rebut this. By claiming that the truth of an opinion is part of its utility, he in fact tries to undermine the two-level analysis above. Mill would say that in order to find out whether q is true, one has to know whether or not p is true. One can't have a rational assurance that q is true unless one is free to discuss the truth or falsity of p. So one has to allow freedom to discuss both p and q. But surely Mill goes too far here. For it is possible, and perhaps even likely, that in the sort of situation under consideration, whether or not p is true, dangerous consequences will result from its expression.

Mill himself recognizes the dangers of free speech in certain situations. He says that 'even opinions lose their immunity when the circumstances in which they are expressed are such as to constitute their expression a positive instigation to some mischievous act.' (p. 114.) Thus one may prevent the opinion that corn-dealers are starvers of the poor from being delivered orally to an excited crowd assembled in front of the corn-dealer's house. But the same opinion should be permitted to be expressed in the press. Again he believes that the instigation to tyrannicide 'in a specific case, may be a proper subject of punishment, but only if an overt act has followed, and at least a probable connection can be established between the act and the instigation' (p. 78).

Although Mill uses the same term 'instigation', his two cases are different in some important respects. In the tyrannicide example, it would appear that the resultant harm, the killing of a particular person, must be intended by the speaker or the writer. But in the corn-dealer case, the 'positive instigation' is not of this type: the speaker may neither intend nor even welcome any harm to the corn-dealers, and yet, in the given circumstances, his speech would be a causally relevant factor in bringing about the harm. He need not be urging the excited crowd to commit any 'mischievous act', but none the less harmful acts are very likely to result. The most that one could infer from Mill's description is that the speaker was carelessly indifferent to the fate of the corn-dealer, or that he was unusually stupid in not foreseeing that harm would result from the expression of his view in the given situation.

Because the notion of 'instigation' in the corn-dealer case is a causal and not an intentional concept, it appears that Mill is not confining restrictions to freedom of expression merely to contexts where someone urges others, with the probability of success, to commit specific harmful acts. But there is now a real danger that the restrictions of freedom of expression that are permitted by Mill's remarks in the corn-dealer example may be far greater than he supposes, or would be prepared to accept. As Watkins has argued,

But suppose that the publication of a certain book may reasonably be expected to lead, after a time-lag, to much more serious damage than would have been caused by the speech outside the corn-dealer's house: would not society be justified, on Mill's principles, in suppressing such a book? Or consider the series of scientific papers which made possible the construction of an atom-bomb: should not they have been suppressed?[6]

The way out for Mill is to insist, as his corn-dealer case suggests, on the immediacy of the harm done by the expression of an opinion before that opinion can be legitimately suppressed. This rules out an appeal to harm that may arise in the long run, and thereby confines restrictions on freedom of expression to a relatively small class. But what considerations favour this proposal?

First, there are the familiar uncertainties about making long-term predictions. Again, where no immediate damage is likely, we have the oppotunity of bringing into play the good effects that discussion generally has: dangerous opinions can be argued against and countered with other views. Even if there is every reason to believe that serious long-term harm will result from the expression of an opinion, our very awareness of this, and our continued attempts to argue against the opinion or to avert the harm, may be enough. This at least would be the belief, or sometimes perhaps merely the hope, of a Millian liberal.

In certain cases his hope will indeed prove to be too

optimistic. But the alternative policy of allowing the state the right to suppress free speech, whenever it can put up a reasonable case that such expression will cause long-term damage to society, is highly undesirable. Even when the state allows its decisions to be openly challenged, this will not be enough to remove the grave threat to the atmosphere of free inquiry inherent in the conferring of such a right. In the nature of the case, new and bold, as well as old and unpopular, ideas are likely to look dangerous to most people, and the state will have no difficulty in putting up a reasonable case, acceptable to the majority, that serious harm will be caused by the open espousal of such ideas.

Part of the apparent reasonableness of the state's case will depend on the fact that the harmful ideas may threaten a change in the existing legal rights of persons, and thus be subversive of the current social order.

Furthermore, a man's conception of what constitutes harm tends to be partly determined by the prevailing framework of accepted ideas. And this raises a fundamental difference between, on the one hand, the claim that immediate harm will result from the expression of an opinion, and on the other hand the claim that serious long-term harm will be caused. In the short run if free speech leads to a violation of accepted legal rights of persons, this will constitute the damage done. But the violation in the distant future of current legal rights need not be regarded as harm viewed from the perspective of a changed legal and social order. The legal rights of persons change with time, and some of these rights may cease to exist, and hence may no longer be there to be violated. So there is a conceptual problem in predicting that certain types of damage would result in the long run from the expression of particular opinions. Consider Mill's own example of someone expressing the view that private property is theft. If this is delivered before an excited crowd which immediately proceeds to steal the goods of wealthy people, then these acts of theft would be the harm resulting from the expression of the opinion. But if, on the other hand, it is claimed that no such immediate effects are forthcoming, but that far more serious cases of theft will result in the long run from the constant utterances of this opinion, one may object that if the run is indeed a very long one, private property may by then have been abolished by constitutional changes. No 'stealing' is possible without the institution of private property, and hence no harm of this type can be inflicted. One has, however, to be careful not to exaggerate this point. It applies to certain types of damage or harm that are closely bound up with the violation of a particular system of values embodied in a definite social or legal order. It does not apply equally to harm that consists in the violation of the physical integrity of the person, for here the concept of harm seems to be tied to something more general and fundamental than variable social orders. Unless human beings become very different from what they now are, physical assault will cause harm in any social system, and hence speech that leads men to assault other persons physically will be harmful in the same sense, whether or not the harm is caused in the immediate or in the distant future.[7]

Again where the harmful effect follows immediately from the expression of a certain view, the expression is often so closely connected with the act as to be properly considered part of the act. Any description of what happened would be incomplete unless it incorporated the expression. This is particularly so in the case of verbal expressions urging an immediate and specific harmful act, and delivered to a live audience face to face.[8]

Finally, the further away the harmful consequences are from the time of the expression, the more likely it is that there are other intervening causal factors which contribute to the harm. The imputation of responsibility cannot then be fairly laid on the agent's expression. The intervention of other factors lets him off the hook.

Though the likelihood of immediate harm is a necessary condition of justifiable legal intervention, it is not always a sufficient condition. There are other relevant factors. It matters, for example, whether the agent was responsible for the resultant harm, or whether he was a victim of a deliberate and organized disruption of public order by an intolerant section of his audience who wished to prevent his unpopular view from being heard.[9]

Mill himself pays little attention to the circumstances

under which freedom of expression may justifiably be restricted.[10] The corn-dealer example is mentioned only in passing, and the incitement to tyrannicide is discussed in a footnote. He is much more concerned with putting forward the theoretical grounds for freedom of expression in general. His liberal theory is incomplete unless it is supplemented with a more detailed examination of the types of restrictions which it would allow. But such a detailed examination should follow from a clearer appreciation of the nature of the general theory. For Mill the chief justification of freedom of expression is that it enables even persons of ordinary intellect to strive to know the truth and thereby to attain 'the dignity of thinking beings'.[11] This ideal of what a worthwhile human life should be is, he feels, within the reach of ordinary persons in many areas of their lives. It is of course the same ideal of individuality that he is here appealing to. The ideal underlies and unifies both his case for freedom of expression and that for freedom of action.

The scope of Mill's defence of freedom of expression does not cover the dissemination of information, whether true or false, about a person's private life which has no bearing on the scientific, moral, political, religious, and social issues with which he is concerned. Although Mill regards freedom of expression as belonging to 'that part of the conduct of an individual which concerns other people', he makes a strong plea for 'the fullest liberty of professing and discussing, as a matter of ethical conviction, any doctrine, however immoral it may be considered' (p. 78). While this does not amount to a demand for absolute freedom of expression, it carries with it implications hostile to attempts to suppress any doctrine simply on the ground that it is unacceptable to a group of people, or to the majority, or even to 'all mankind minus one'. For example, the suppression of views simply because they are regarded as blasphemous and obscene would not be justified. If we regard blasphemous and obscene remarks as expressions of opinion, then they must come under the protection accorded freedom of speech. In the absence of any clear harm, there is no case for their suppression.

The case against using the law to suppress blasphemy is particularly clear. In its essence blasphemy involves the expression of an opinion that others find outrageous, shocking, or offensive because it treats, or is regarded as treating, disrespectfully or contemptuously what others regard as sacred. In the end there is no particular reason why blasphemy should be confined to religious matters. Certainly a staunchly religious man is likely to be offended by certain remarks directed at, or ridiculing, his religion. But what a person finds shocking depends on what he deeply cherishes, and religion is not the only subject about which people feel strongly. Indeed a recent commentator suggests: 'Religion and sexuality have lost much of their old power to shock. But the capacity for being shocked has not evaporated; it has simply attached itself, for an energetic minority at any rate, to a new subject-matter.'[12] According to him this new subject-matter is race relations, and he refers in particular to Mr Enoch Powell's views on coloured immigrants. However, the persistent censorship of obscene and pornographic books, and the recent prosecution of *Gay News* and its editor for blasphemous libel,[13] help to remind us that religion and sexuality have lost their power to shock only as far as many liberals and radicals are concerned, but that there is still a sizeable group for whom religious and sexual matters are still the sources of deep offence.

So we are confronted with a situation in which many liberals and radicals are deeply angered and shocked by racist remarks and want to use the law to suppress them, whereas many politically conservative people argue against such suppression by invoking the general right to free speech. On the other hand, these same liberals and radicals are against the censorship of obscenity and blasphemy. If there is an inconsistency in their attitudes, this inconsistency is equally evident in the views of those who firmly believe that blasphemy should be a crime, while at the same time preaching the right of people to express racist views. Both sides seem to have been carried away by the strength of their respective feelings, and to have abandoned all firm principles.

Maurice Cranston has argued that, 'only a society with no values at all — only a society with no sense of the sacred — could fail to be sensitive to blasphemy; an unshockable society would be unbearably barbarous.'[14] Although Cranston thinks that the penalty imposed in the *Gay News* case was too severe, he does not wish to remove blasphemy as a crime. But the argument he gives is unacceptable. A society can be 'sensitive to blasphemy' in the sense of being shocked by it, without at the same time wishing to invoke the criminal law to suppress what it finds shocking. Such a society will resist the step from being shocked to suppression simply because it places a high value on the freedom of individuals to express their opinions. Moreover, different persons are shocked by different things, and who can doubt that what shocked Mrs Mary Whitehouse did not in fact shock many others? So the case for retaining the crime of blasphemy is reduced either to the claim that the majority in a society has the right not to be shocked, or else to the view that whatever shocks any sizeable group of persons may be suppressed.

The former view might not support the decision in *Gay News* because it is certainly arguable that the poem the magazine printed would not have shocked a majority in the society. But even if Mrs Whitehouse were in the majority, it would still be wrong to punish the magazine and its editor. Such punishment will confer on the majority a right not to have its cherished institutions and views ridiculed or strongly criticized. It will thereby entrench orthodoxies. On another occasion, Cranston himself has drawn attention to what he called a new kind of 'secular blasphemy', and I quote his admirable remarks:

One of the reasons given for the suppression of Pasternak's novel *Dr. Zhivago* was that the author wrote disrespectfully of the achievements of the Bolshevik Revolution. There have been cases in Greece of writers being imprisoned for speaking disrespectfully of the military regime. The offence in such cases is that of writing in an impudent or insolent fashion about what is thought to be sacred and to require veneration. The offence may not be call 'blasphemy', but that is what it comes down to; and the more secular institutions are allowed to claim divinity, the more widespread this offence is likely to become in future.[15]

But if a majority of Christians is allowed to suppress what it finds shocking, so too would a majority of communists, fascists, conservatives, racists, puritans, etc.

The other basis for making blasphemy a crime — that it shocks a sizeable group of people — fares no better. No doubt it has the advantage of removing a certain partiality towards the majority, of which the existing law is guilty. As a leading article in *The Times* pointed out, the common law offence of blasphemy is confined solely to attacks on Christianity.[16] Other religious groups are rightly aggrieved by this obvious unfairness. But the law will still be unfair if we extend the crime of blasphemy to cover the religions of substantial minorities. For if one is justified in making blasphemy a crime simply because substantial minorities are shocked by blasphemous remarks, then why is it that the law should only protect *religious* groups? Substantial political, social, racial, or sexual minorities may be shocked as much as religious minorities by hostile comments. If all of them have their sensitivities protected by the law, then there is little that anyone can say which will not run foul of the law.

A curious feature of the recent discussion of blasphemy is a failure not only to see this general point, but also a more specific failure to appreciate the fact that if there is to be a crime of blasphemy at all, then basic requirements of fairness demand that atheists, agnostics, and humanists should receive the protection of the law against blasphemy just as much as Christians, or any other religious group with a substantial number of adherents. *The Times* argued for the placing of Muslims, Hindus, Sikhs, Buddhists, and Jews on the same footing as Christians, but it failed to raise its voice for the large numbers of non-believers who too can be shocked or offended by the vilification and attacks on them and their views.[17] Atheists are regularly subjected to attacks by religious groups not only for specific 'immoralities', but also for their general incapacity for acting morally because of the alleged dependence of morality on religion.

There can therefore be no justification of a law against blasphemy which is grounded simply in the claim of people to be protected from what shocks them. We know that once we accept freedom of speech, shocking opinions of one type or another will be expressed. Of course there are occasions on which the manner of expression of such opinions is likely to cause definite harm to others, or a breach of the peace. On such occasions restrictions are justifiable, not to suppress the opinions as such, but to regulate their manner of expression.

Thus a group of white racists who march through a predominantly coloured neighbourhood carrying racist placards and shouting racist slogans, may be stopped. By the same token, we may prevent a person from shouting blasphemous remarks outside a church where people are gathered for a service. This kind of regulation of free speech is acceptable, but it requires no distinctive crime of blasphemy for its implementation. However, it is wrong to punish blasphemous remarks in a book or journal which no religious person is required to read. Similarly, racist remarks in the same media should be permitted unless one can distinguish between the two types of cases by showing that racist statements cause definite harm as distinguished from strong offence. In other words, one may be justified in suppressing racist remarks on the ground that they cause racial bashings or unlawful racial discrimination in, for example, jobs and housing. But one is never justified in suppressing such remarks simply because they offend a significant group of people, or even the overwhelming majority in a society.

So far I have discussed the right to make blasphemous remarks as part of the general right to free speech. But it may now be argued that blasphemous remarks cannot really be brought under the protection of free speech. It is obvious that for the argument to get off the ground, the offence of blasphemy must be construed much more narrowly that I have construed it. It may be suggested that what is to be censored are blasphemous remarks which are not merely shocking, but which also fail to have any weighty or serious 'redeeming social value'. The same argument has been used against obscene books. It is one thing to express an opinion, no matter how disgusting and offensive it may be to others; but it is quite another thing to make profane and obscene remarks in a manner that is not at all essential to the expression of any opinion. Such remarks are gratuitous, and gratuitously shocking, and that, it is argued, is the justification for suppressing their public utterance.

This kind of defence of censorship has been well developed in the fight against 'hard-core' pornography, and I shall now turn my attention to this area. A typical hard-core pornographic book will have the following features:

(i) its content is quite explicitly and crudely about sexual matters; (ii) its author has the intention of sexually arousing or stimulating his readers; and (iii) it has no intrinsic literary or other scholarly merit, though there is disagreement about whether or not it is useful in, for example, sexual therapy. I do not of course imply that a pornographic book has no entertainment value. But it has no value over and above this, in the way that a work of art or a sociological investigation is valuable. A pornographic book should therefore be distinguished from those literary works which are 'obscene' in the sense of containing offensive passages about sexual matters.

Now it is part of the conventional wisdom that such works of art, and other works of scholarly interest, should be accepted, whereas pornographic books should be severely censored. The development of the obscenity laws in the English-speaking world may be viewed as an attempt to give increasingly rational articulation to the conventional wisdom. Thus a book must be judged as a whole and not in isolated passages, and the testimonies of literary experts and other scholars are relevant. However, there is an old tradition of thought which believes that works of art are likely to have undesirable or harmful effects, and this has permeated to some extent into the general social consciousness. So it is no part of the conventional wisdom that once a book has passed literary muster, it should be allowed an unrestricted circulation. The literary merit of a book must be weighed against the possibly harmful effects the book may have. But in this balancing of values, art and the interests of scholarship at least get independent recognition.

On the other hand, the conventional wisdom is very intolerant of pornography. Since a pornographic book has no literary or other scholarly merit, it needs very little to tip the scales in favour of censorship. This, I think, in part explains why the arguments for censorship have often been so feeble. For if censorship violates no important social value, then it is unnecessary to put up a strong case in its favour. Cries of moral indignation, and vague allusions to the corruption and destruction of the social fabric are sufficient.

Those who are against the censorship of pornographic

books have usually fallen back on one of the following three types of argument.

(1) It is conceded that the reading of pornographic books will have some harmful effects, but it is maintained that censorship will only increase the harmful effects by whetting men's appetite for forbidden fruits. In non-totalitarian countries it is impossible to wipe out the trade in pornographic books. But to drive pornography underground, without being able to suppress it sufficiently, will only give it a dangerous glamour.

(2) The reading of pornographic books has neither good nor bad effects, but is itself a pleasurable experience. The pleasure it gives outweighs the offence to others.

(3) The reading of pornographic books has positively good effects in, for example, reducing sexual crimes. It does not drive men to commit sexual crimes, but is instead a substitute for such crimes. It is a safety-valve that lets off excess sexual energy which would otherwise be channelled into harmful conduct.

But these arguments, by confining the issue entirely to the effects of reading pornography, tend to lose sight of a fundamental principle. For it must not be assumed that the fact that pornography lacks the value of scholarly works, and the fact that it offends a significant number of people, in any way constitute a prima-facie case against its toleration. We need not justify our activities to others just because they regard them as valueless and are offended by them. What is at stake here is the place of toleration in social life.

On one view, toleration of different beliefs and practices is justified because the truth is thereby promoted or enriched. Hence if pornographic books are to be tolerated, they must, like scholarly works, contribute in some way to the enlargement of our knowledge. If they fail to do so, then the only reason for tolerating them is that the social cost of intolerance is greater than that of tolerance.

But to defend toleration solely on this basis is to be content with Mill's Avoidance of Mistake Argument and to ignore the rest of his case for freedom of expression. There is also a different basis for toleration, and it is here that the example of religious toleration is instructive. For whatever may have been the case at other times and in other places, the present proliferation of religious and quasi-religious sects makes it less likely that each new sect brings with it some fresh vision of the spiritual life. In his classic *Letter Concerning Toleration*, Locke argued passionately for religious toleration in spite of his conviction of the truth of Christianity. Similarly, many advocates of religious toleration today would also claim that as far as they are concerned, their religion contains all the relevant truth, and other religions, in so far as they put forward incompatible views, are false, and perhaps even perverse and degrading. If their acknowledgement of the value of religious toleration does not rest on social and political expediency, then it seems likely that they are committed to something like Mill's ideal of individuality, or some similar ideal of man as an autonomous or self-determining being, pursuing his own good as he sees it, and controlled by his own standards of how he ought to behave. They will recognize that in the absence of harm to others, they are not entitled to dictate to a person how he should express himself to a willing audience.

The case for tolerating activities that offend us does not therefore depend on whether we think that these activities are valuable, over and above the satisfaction of people's obvious desire freely to engage in them. Religious toleration is widely accepted today, but a principled commitment to religious toleration carries with it the toleration of all activities which merely offend us. It is for this reason that the real enemies of 'our way of life' and some of our most cherished values are not the blasphemers and the producers and consumers of pornography, but rather all those who refuse to tolerate what they find merely offensive, disgusting, and of no value.

9

Mill and Liberty

I. INTRODUCTION

The great interest shown in Mill's moral and political philosophy in recent years has produced some illuminating results. In moral philosophy he has been rescued from some of the crude mistakes attributed to him. In political philosophy the results have been less clear, but there is an increasing belief that the essay *On Liberty* is a more complex piece of work than is generally supposed. Until very recently, however, both critics and admirers of the essay have never doubted that it is a defence of individual liberty. They disagreed about its value, but not about its liberal intentions. But even this unanimity has now been broken with the publication of Maurice Cowling's *Mill and Liberalism*,[1] a fierce repudiation of Mill, who is accused of 'more than a touch of something resembling moral totalitarianism', and of intellectual 'jealousy, and a carefully disguised intolerance'. In his comprehensive attack, Cowling does not spare the essay *On Liberty*, which is, according to him, only superficially a sustained plea for individual liberty. The individuality Mill defends is a selective one: it is the individuality of the elevated, and Mill's doctrine is really designed to detract from human freedom, and not to maximize it. The evidence Cowling accumulates to support his interpretation of Mill stretches over a very long period of Mill's life, from the early essays of 1831 on *The Spirit of the Age* to his Inaugural Address to the University of St. Andrews, delivered in 1867, and the posthumously published *Three Essays on Religion*. Cowling's account of Mill is supported to some extent by Shirley Letwin. In the section on Mill in *The Pursuit of Certainty*,[2] Letwin does not go so far as Cowling in her assertion of illiberalism in Mill. She sees Mill as divided between 'two incompatible ends'. Mill according to her,

marked the birth of the 'liberal intellectual', so familiar today, who with one part of him genuinely values liberty and recognizes the equal

144

right of all adults to decide their lives for themselves, but with another wants the government, under the direction of the superior few, to impose what he considers the good life on all his fellows.[3]

None the less Cowling can draw some support from Letwin, for she seems to regard the illiberal side of Mill as the truer one, and it is certainly the side which she emphasizes even in the context of her discussion of the essay *On Liberty*.

Another interesting, though different, study of Mill is that of Gertrude Himmelfarb.[4] She does not doubt that the essay *On Liberty* is a defence of individual liberty, but she warns us not to be overwhelmed by it, for there was another Mill 'who wrote in quite a different vein and was anything but the perfect liberal'. The Mill of the essay *On Liberty* had an intellectual life of less than two decades, starting in the 1840s and culminating in *On Liberty*. The other Mill is the Mill of the 1830s and the Mill who broke loose again after the death of his wife, Harriet Taylor, in 1858.

Himmelfarb has also devoted an entire book, *On Liberty and Liberalism*,[5] to a development of her thesis about the two Mills. But, as we shall see, her account of the other Mill in the book differs from, and is inconsistent with, her earlier version in some important respects.

What then is the truth of the matter? In this chapter, I shall argue that the traditional view of Mill as a liberal is fundamentally correct, though I shall distinguish three different phases in the development of his ideas on liberty. I shall maintain that both Cowling's and Himmelfarb's accounts of Mill are mistaken, Cowling's almost completely, and Himmelfarb's to a lesser extent. Although Cowling's case will be considered first, I shall discuss Himmelfarb's views at much greater length. Her more discriminating studies of Mill are likely to seem more persuasive.[6]

II. COWLING'S MILL

The falsity of Cowling's picture of Mill is most conspicuous in his short chapter on the essay *On Liberty*. He concedes that at first sight the essay seems to be more liberal and individualistic than he is prepared to allow; he concedes that Mill's notion of self-regarding actions appears to limit the area of interference with individual conduct; he concedes further that Mill pleads for non-interference 'for the sake of the greater good of human freedom'; but he still succeeds in concluding that 'On Liberty does not offer safeguards for *individuality*; it is designed to propagate the individuality of the elevated by protecting them against the mediocrity of opinion as a whole.'[7] If Cowling merely means that Mill prefers one type of personality to another, he is surely right, but then Mill's advocacy of individual liberty is in no way compromised. A Christian is not illiberal if he prefers Christianity to all other religions, so long as he is prepared to allow others their freedom of worship. Cowling seems to make the tacit assumption that the holding of any substantive doctrine, the support of any group in society, is *ipso facto* a renunciation of a belief in individual liberty. It is only on this assumption that he can profess to find any incompatibility between Mill's liberalism and his belief in the Religion of Humanity or in the 'elevated individuality'. Thus in one place, when he is considering Mill's discussion of Comte's views, Cowling argues that Mill's ethical injunctions leave no room for the belief that there could be more than one road to human happiness, for Mill is saying that 'there is a doctrine, one doctrine, defining the nature of happiness and the means to achieve it, and that that doctrine is binding.'[8] Cowling is thus able to play down, or even completely ignore, the many passages in the essay *On Liberty* where Mill defends different 'experiments in living' and explicitly denies that liberty is desired for the 'elevated' alone. Thus Mill writes:

I have said that it is important to give the freest scope possible to uncustomary things, in order that it may in time appear which of these are fit to be converted into customs. But independence of action, and disregard of custom, are not solely deserving of encouragement for the chance they afford that better modes of action, and customs more worthy of general adoption, may be struck out; *nor is it only persons of decided mental superiority who have a just claim to carry on their lives in their own way.* There is no reason that all human existence should be constructed on some one or small number of patterns. If a person possesses any tolerable amount of common sense and experience, his own mode of laying out his existence is the best, not because it is the best in itself, but because it is his own mode. (*My italics.*)[9]

Letwin makes the same mistakes when she says that '*On Liberty* was not a defence of the common man's right to live as he liked; it was more nearly an attack on him.'[10] There is no doubt that Mill preferred one type of personality to others. He admired the man who had 'character', who could think for himself. He criticized very strongly those who followed custom blindly and mechanically, who merely displayed 'the ape-like' faculty of imitation; but he did not claim that they had no right to live as they liked. Nor did he provide what Letwin accuses him of, namely, 'a justification of withholding personal liberty from any claimant unable to demonstrate that he was pursuing the "right" ideal and was possessed of sufficient will power to pursue it steadily and energetically'.[11] He believed, or at least hoped, that in conditions of freedom men would think for themselves, and order their actions according to their own conceptions of what is good or bad, under the guidance but not the dictatorship of customs and traditions, and with the experience and wisdom of others. But if, having been freed from the imposed tyranny of custom, they still voluntarily submitted themselves to it blindly, or failed to live up to the ideal of rationality, there is no evidence in the essay *On Liberty* to indicate that Mill would deny them their right to live as they wished, so long as their conduct was not harmful to others, though there is much evidence to show that he would indeed be contemptuous of them. Mill denied that we had the right to compel the Mormons 'to conform to the opinions of other people' even though he strongly disapproved of their institution of polygamy, and felt that it was a 'retrograde step in civilisation'.[12] His reason for this is that 'all who are directly interested appear to be satisfied.' In promoting his own ideals of personal excellence Mill is committed to argument and persuasion, and not force and coercion. Letwin is sometimes aware of this, but she allows it to slip too easily into the language of 'imposition' and intolerance.

Mill explicitly rejects the assumption that tolerance of another implies complete indifference to his behaviour. Coercion and the use of 'whips and scourges, either of the literal or metaphorical sort' are ruled out, but 'Considerations to aid his judgement, exhortations to strengthen his will, may be offered to him, by others: but he himself is the

final judge.'[13] A liberal does not cease to believe in individual
liberty just because he holds certain substantive doctrines or
standards of human excellence, or because he attempts to
propagate them by argument and persuasion. He is to be
distinguished by his belief that these doctrines and standards
should not be imposed on others who should be free to choose
for themselves, and Mill clearly passes the test.

Mill's acceptance of the idea of clerisy of superior minds
is also misrepresented by Cowling. He is aware that Mill
strongly opposed Comte's 'spiritual despotism', and he mentions the fact that for Mill the moral consensus should not
be arbitrary or imposed. But at the same time he speaks of
Mill's assumption that 'the subject of study—Man in Society—
can be successfully pursued only so far as the higher rational
impulses, imposing themselves on the lower ones, help to
bring this unity about.'[14] If Cowling accepts the fact that
Mill rules out the use of coercion, how can be consistently
maintain that the higher impulses are to *impose* themselves
on the lower ones? Mill's liberalism never led him to deny
that some men are wiser and nobler than others. But he did
not believe that the wiser and nobler men have the right to
compel or coerce others. In the essay *On Liberty* he addresses
himself explicitly to this point, and comes out clearly in
favour of individual liberty. The enlightened can claim the
right to point out the way but 'the power of compelling
others into it is not only inconsistent with the freedom and
development of all the rest, but corrupting to the strong
man himself.'[15] If this much is clear, then the notion of a
clerisy in Mill's hands need not have authoritarian implications. The equality of intellects was never accepted by
Mill. There was always a place in his system of thought for
superior minds, but the role he envisaged for them was not
a tyrannical one, at least in the essay *On Liberty*. Cowling,
however, makes it appear to be otherwise by his constant
emphasis on the fact that Mill believed that ultimately there
would be a universal consensus. He apparently believes that
the acceptance of such a consensus somehow reduces the
significance of Mill's commitment to individual freedom,
for he says:

Whatever the means Mill advocates in order to achieve solidarity and

and rational participation, there can be no doubt, and there is no ambiguity about the fact, that he believes this to be a proper function of human society: and there is, beyond the libertarian character of the means, an assumption of the fundamental homogeneity of all rational judgement.[16]

If the suggestion here is that Mill only accepts freedom because it is an effective means of bringing about a rational consensus, and would reject it if there were other more effective means, then nothing can be further from the truth. Mill's fundamental objection to Comte's way of arriving at the consensus is not that it is ineffective, but that it is coercive and incolves the surrender of individual freedom. Thus in a letter to Harriet Taylor of 15 January 1855, Mill says that 'opinion tends to encroach more and more on liberty, and almost all the projects of social reformers of these days are really *liberticide* — Comte, particularly so',[17] and in his detailed discussion of Comte's doctrines in *August Comte and Positivism,* this is the criticism to which he returns again and again. If Mill regards the achievement of a consensus as of overriding importance, and freedom as to be valued only so long as it achieves this end, it would be difficult to explain why he should object so strongly to the suppression of individual liberty as a means of achieving unanimity of opinion. The consensus Cowling speaks of is acceptable to Mill only if it is obtained without suppressing individual freedom. Mill believed that individual freedom and the consensus of opinion are compatible.

Cowling seems to imply that if they are not compatible, Mill would sacrifice individual freedom. But there is no evidence to support this, and much to suggest the opposite view that Mill would in fact reject the consensus simply because it is imposed and as such undesirable.

It is difficult to see why Cowling places so much emphasis on Mill's belief in an ultimate consensus. Does he think that once the consensus is obtained freedom is no longer desirable to Mill? If so, he is quite wrong. Mill accepted the Saint-Simonian division of history into organic and critical periods. In an organic period there is some positive doctrine which is generally accepted and guides human behaviour. But in time the organic period gives way to a critical period when men reject the old doctrine without at the same time replacing it by another. The critical period is one of scepticism and criticism. Mill believes that in such a period new opinions are likely to get a good hearing, but the critical period does not last for ever, and sooner or later a new doctrine will dominate men's minds; a new consensus is achieved. But in the *Autobiography* Mill states that it is in such a period, where there is a dominating doctrine, that 'the teachings of the "Liberty" will have their greatest value'.[18] He valued freedom not only in the critical but also in the organic period. While he welcomed an ultimate consensus on many issues he at the same time

looked forward, through the present age of loud disputes but generally weak convictions, to a future which shall unite the best qualities of the critical with the best qualities of the organic periods; unchecked liberty of thought, unbounded freedom of individual action in all modes not hurtful to others; . . .[19]

Freedom is not for Mill merely a means to an end which may be discarded once the end is achieved. Freedom is a permanent part of Mill's system of beliefs. It is the only desirable means to the achievement of consensus, and its continued presence after consensus is obtained is what keeps that consensus desirable.

Cowling makes one more attempt to support his accusation of illiberalism and intolerance in Mill. Referring to Mill's Inaugural Address to the University of St. Andrews, where he had spoken of the importance of 'general culture,' Cowling asserts:

General Culture means . . . critical reflection and mental doubt, sceptical scrutiny of existing habits, and, where habits are judged to be irrational or wrong, deciding which habits shall replace them. It means *following the argument whithersoever it leads us*; . . . It means, in short, moral indoctrination . . .[20]

Mill, according to Cowling, supposed indoctrination to be the chief function of a university. Cowling may wish to define critical reflection and freedom of inquiry as moral indoctrination, but why should he suppose that this has anything to do with Mill? Cowling writes:

Any set of general principles excludes some other set; any set of intellectual injunctions involves rejection of many others. *Freedom of enquiry* is an intellectual injunction, which inhibits commitment to injunctions hostile to it.[21]

In a sense this is trivially true. If one is for freedom of inquiry, one must be against the imposition of a particular substantive doctrine in the sense that one wants it suppressed. Freedom of inquiry is a procedural injunction and is compatible with the existence of several conflicting substantive doctrines. Mill believed that the purpose of education is not to inculcate a particular doctrine which is now accepted as true, but to train men to think for themselves, and to judge for themselves what is true or what is right.[22] The belief that men should be trained to think and judge for themselves will of course be indirectly opposed to some substantive doctrines which are so irrational that they can be accepted only blindly and unthinkingly. Mill had confidence in his own substantive doctrines. Cowling, however, sometimes picks on this very confidence as a sign of illiberalism, as if Mill would not accept freedom of inquiry if he thought that this would lead to the rejection of his substantive doctrines like the Religion of Humanity. But surely Mill's arguments for freedom of discussion show that if his own doctrines do not survive freedom of inquiry, then they are false, and they, not freedom of inquiry, should be discarded.

Though Cowling may sometimes catch a fleeting glimpse of the truth about Mill, the total picture which emerges from his book is false and misleading. To get at the tiny element of truth in it, one has to be more discriminating about the different periods in Mill's life. For this one has to turn to Himmelfarb.

III. HIMMELFARB'S TWO MILLS

Himmelfarb does not try to show that *On Liberty* is not a liberal tract. She regards the essay as the culmination of the 'later' Mill, as she calls him, and contrasts its doctrines with those of the other or 'earlier' Mill. She believes that the 'earlier' Mill has been overlooked because Mill's biographers have been overwhelmed by *On Liberty*, and because Mill himself rewrote his own past in his *Autobiography*. The greater part of the *Autobiography* was written concurrently with the essay *On Liberty* and both works were closely supervised by Harriet Taylor. Mill's selection and editing of *Dissertations and Discussions*, in which again his wife shared, also distorted the picture of his intellectual development. He made significant alterations in his essay which did not appear in their original versions. Himmelfarb has edited a valuable collection of Mill's essays which, according to her, shows the 'earlier' Mill. Some of these essays belong to the period 1831–1840, while the rest are drawn from the period after Harriet's death in 1858, when Mill, she claims, 'reverted to the philosophical temper of the earlier period'. Himmelfarb presents some earlier essays, which were reprinted in *Dissertations and Discussions,* not as they appeared there but in their original versions. In various footnotes she meticulously indicates those changes made by Mill in his edition of the essays in *Dissertations and Discussions* 'that alter the sense or the tone of the original'.

In trying to assess the correctness of Himmelfarb's account of the 'earlier' Mill, one faces the problem that the contrast between this Mill and the 'later' Mill is not always well defined. Sometimes the 'earlier' Mill is represented as the Mill who retreated from radicalism, and at other times he is represented as the illiberal Mill who rejected the doctrines of the essay *On Liberty.* These two versions of the 'earlier' Mill need not coincide, for it is not at all clear that the rejection of specific doctrines held by the philosophic Radicals is necessarily a repudiation of a strong belief in individual liberty. Since my purpose is only to consider Mill's views on individual liberty, I shall discuss whether the evidence given by Himmelfarb is sufficient to support her thesis about an 'earlier' Mill who was at odds with the teachings of the essay *On Liberty.*

I shall consider first the evidence for the claim that after Harriet Taylor's death Mill once more propounded doctrines inconsistent with those of the essay *On Liberty.* Here I think that Himmelfarb's case is at its weakest, for her two versions of the 'earlier' Mill now come apart most clearly. The examples she gives of Mill's retreat from radicalism — his acceptance of the ideas of plural voting and proportional representation — do not seem to me to deviate from anything he said in *On Liberty*. Indeed Himmelfarb also mentions his fears of the tyranny of the majority, and on this important point there is surely no change from the essay *On Liberty*. There he put forward his 'one very simple principle' to protect individuals from the tyranny of the majority. Now he is proposing other safeguards against the same tyranny he feared so much, though he does not seem to accord them the same status as the 'simple principle'. They were not held as absolute principles, but more as devices which facilitate the ventilation of minority views. Mill was not against giving power to the numerical majority, but he was profoundly afraid that it would get all the power. In his *Autobiography* he maintains:

Minorities, so long as they remain minorities, are, and ought to be, outvoted; but under arrangements which enable any assemblage of voters, amounting to a certain number, to place in the legislature representatives of its own choice, minorities cannot be suppressed. Independent opinions will force their way into the council of the nation and make themselves heard there, a thing which often cannot happen in the existing forms of representative democracy; and the legislature, instead of being weeded of individual peculiarities and entirely made up of men who simply represent the creed of great political or religious parties, will comprise a large proportion of the most eminent individual minds in the country, placed there, without reference to party, by voters who appreciate their individual eminency.[23]

However objectionable his proposals about plural voting and proportional representation may have been to the Radicals, the fact is that these proposals were designed primarily to ensure that minority opinions were given the opportunity of being heard. As such they are not incompatible with anything Mill said in the essay *On Liberty*.

At one point, however, Himmelfarb specifically contrasts *Considerations on Representative Government* with *On Liberty*. *Representative Government* is 'subtle and complex' and shows no yearning for a 'single truth' or 'one very simple principle'.[24] But I am afraid that I fail to see the point of the alleged contrast. If Mill's liberty principle is 'very simple', then so are some of his *conclusions* in *Representative Government*, such as the idea of plural voting. And there are probably 'subtle and complex' arguments in both works. But setting these aside, I do not understand how the 'one very simple principle' of *On Liberty* is in any way compromised by the 'subtle and complex inquiry' in *Representative Government*. As for Mill's concern in the latter work with limiting the power of democratic government, this is another manifestation of his fear of the tyranny of the majority, which also permeates the essay *On Liberty*.

In her book *On Liberty and Liberalism*, Himmelfarb contrasts Mill's proposals on proportional representation and plural voting, as propounded in *Representative Government* and *Thoughts on Parliamentary Reform* (1859), with his views in the essay *On Liberty*. Whereas in these two works his proposals give an 'unequal voice' to different people, and he is convinced that 'one person is not as good as another',[25] in *On Liberty* he takes the entirely different line, 'that every person, every opinion, and every expression of individuality was "as good as another" '.[26] But this is a distortion of Mill's defence of individual liberty. To argue against the use of coercion in preventing a person from expressing his opinion, or from developing his individuality, is not to be committed to the very different view that one opinion or one way of life is just as good as another. Mill does not go back on his view in *On Liberty* that the wise should only persuade, but not compel, the unwise to accept their more enlightened views and way of life. Indeed in *Representative Government*, Mill's criterion of a good government is its ability to promote 'the virtue and intelligence of the people themselves'.[27] It is on this basis that he explicitly rejects government by a 'good despot': 'What should we then have? One man of superhuman mental activity managing the entire affairs of a mentally passive people.'[28] Here, as in *On Liberty*, Mill is concerned to promote conditions congenial to the cultivation of 'intellectually active people'. What he fears is the stunting of men's intellectual and moral capacities, and a good despotism is likely to do this more than a bad one: 'Evil for evil, a good despotism, in a country at all advanced in civilization, is more noxious than a bad one; for it is far more relaxing and enervating to the thoughts, feelings, and energies of the people.'[29]

As far as the period after Harriet Taylor's death in 1858 is concerned, I do not think that Himmelfarb has shown that Mill's views differed from those of *On Liberty*. Indeed in *Auguste Comte and Positivism,* which was written in this period, there is every evidence of a continued belief in individual liberty. For example, he protests that liberty and spontaneity form no part of Comte's scheme,[30] and there is this echo of *On Liberty:*

Why is it necessary that all human life should point but to one object, and be cultivated into a system of means to a single end? May it not be the fact that mankind, who after all are made up of single human beings, obtain a greater sum of happiness when each pursues his own, under the rules and conditions required by the good of the rest, than when each makes the good of the rest his only object and allows himself no personal pleasures not indispensable to the preservation of his faculties.[31]

Let me now turn to the other period involving the 'earlier' Mill. The last essay of this period in Himmelfarb's collection is Mill's second review of Tocqueville's *Democracy in America.* This review was published in October 1840, and Himmelfarb says that it was 'the last of its kind for many years, the end of an epoch in Mill's life'. This period of the 'earlier' Mill ended, therefore, in 1840, and presumably began some time before 9 January 1831, the date of publication of the first part of *The Spirit of the Age,* which is the earliest of Mill's essays in her collection. There is still the Mill of the 1820s, who was already actively publishing, and there were, according to Himmelfarb, also complications in the Mill of the 1830s. She gives a brief description of all these. Until he was twenty Mill was the good son of his father. Then in 1826 he experienced his famous mental crisis, and this led to his being influenced by the writings of Wordsworth, Comte, Carlyle, and Coleridge. Macaulay's attack on his father's *Essay On Government* affected him further, and by 1831 he had already deviated so far from the Radicals and Utilitarians that he could say that all his differences with them, unlike those with any philosophic Tory, were differences of principle. Mill wrote several articles in this new frame of mind but, according to Himmelfarb, his 'awe and fear' of his father made him lead a sort of 'double life'. He wrote articles that would satisfy 'the most fanatical utilitarian and radical'. He thus tried desperately 'to

appease his father while placating his conscience with occasional asides of disagreement'. His father's death in 1836
liberated Mill who, for the next five years, wrote essays
'free from party spirit and partisan purpose'. The essays
on *Civilization, Bentham, Coleridge,* on the *Reorganization
of the Reform Party,* and the second review of Tocqueville,
which are all included in Himmelfarb's collection, belong
to this period. After this Mill came under the dominating
influence of Harriet Taylor and did not revert to the frame
of mind depicted in these essays until after her death.

This, then, is Himmelfarb's picture of Mill from the
1820s to the late 1850s. How true is it? My first difficulty
is with her account of Mill's relationship with his father. I
do not doubt that Mill held his father in some awe, and he
tried to avoid conflicts and disagreements with him. But I
find it difficult to believe that his fear of his father was so
great as to lead him deliberately to publish views at odds with
what he actually believed. He had, after all, stood up to his
father over his friendship with Graham and Roebuck.[32]
It is true that during this period of his life Mill could not
see eye to eye with the Radicals and Utilitarians. But he
still had some sympathies for them. This, combined with his
familiar habit of always presenting the other side of the
picture, is probably a better explanation of those writings of
his which were sympathetic to the Utilitarians than deliberate intellectual dishonesty designed simply to appease his
father.

Himmelfarb's account of the dominating influence of
Harriet Taylor on Mill is also puzzling in some respects. She
does not think much of Harriet personally or intellectually,
but she believes that her influence on Mill was enormous. Mill
first met Harriet in 1830, and in spite of his professions to
the contrary in the *Autobiography,* Himmelfarb is surely
right to claim that 'their relationship became intimate and
confidential almost immediately.'[33] This being the case, why
is it that in Himmelfarb's account Harriet's great influence
on Mill did not show itself until almost a decade later, when
the 'later' Mill emerged in the 1840s? Packe, who also believes
in the dominating influence of Harriet on Mill, dates this
influence from 1832, with the publication of Mill's essay

On Genuis in October of that year. If indeed Harriet's influence was so important, 1832 instead of the 1840s would
have been a more likely date for its manifestation in Mill's
writings. Perhaps Harriet's influence was suppressed by Mill's
fear of his father, but that fear died with James Mill in 1836.
Mill was then free to fall under Harriet's spell, but on Himmelfarb's account did not appear to have done so for another
few years.

In *On Liberty and Liberalism*, Himmelfarb says that in the
first decade of their friendship Harriet did not decisively
influence Mill's thinking. But she now argues that *On Liberty*
conflicts with nearly everything else Mill wrote except the
two essays on women. Whereas the Mill of *On Liberty* propounded and defended the 'one very simple principle' of
liberty, the other Mill was aware of the complexity of social
and political life, and sought to qualify the pursuit of individual liberty with other values, such as 'duty, morality,
discipline, the public good, tradition, community, nationality,
society'.[34] Evidence of the other Mill is now to be found not
only in those periods when Harriet's great influence had
not asserted itself, but also when her influence on Mill was
at its height. The Mill of *On Liberty* is no longer the Mill of
the 1840s and 1850s (up to Harriet's death in 1858) as she
had earlier postulated. The sentiments of the other Mill were
expressed in other writings even at the very time Mill was
working on *On Liberty*.[35] So the Mill of *On Liberty* lives
only in that essay and in the essays on women. As Rees has
pointed out,[36] in the earlier version of the 'two Mills' thesis,
Himmelfarb grouped together *Utilitarianism, Political
Economy,* and *On Liberty* as works not belonging to the
other Mill, but as works produced during the period of
Harriet's greatest influence. But in her book, *Utilitarianism*
and *Political Economy* are included among the works of the
other Mill and set against *On Liberty*.

In *On Liberty and Liberalism,* Himmelfarb argues that Mill
was preoccupied with the question of women's liberation,
and it was this urgent practical issue which led him to formu-
late his principle of liberty: 'the doctrine of liberty was required for the liberation of women.'[37] By showing that men
too, though to a lesser extent, were victims of society's

tyranny, Mill gave both men and women a common interest in promoting individual liberty against the claims of society, custom, and tradition. *On Liberty* was written under the close supervision of Harriet, and her influence pushed him to adopt the absolute value of liberty, an extreme position that contrasted with his customary, moderate mode of thought.

But why is it that Mill's abiding interest in the liberation of women is not reflected in all his writings of the same period when he was under Harriet's strong influence? Himmelfarb gives two reasons. First, the liberation of women is more directly and immediately related to the subject of liberty than it is to the topics Mill dealt with in his other works.[38] Where the cause of women was not directly involved, there was no need to argue a case for absolute freedom, and Mill was able to assume his more usual mode of thought. But this explanation runs counter to her account of the nature of Harriet's influence on Mill. Himmelfarb quotes Mill's remark that in *On Liberty* the 'whole mode of thinking' was Harriet's, and that he too was thoroughly imbued with it.[39] She identifies Harriet's distinctive mode of thought as 'absolutistic and simplistic'. One would therefore expect to see in all of Mill's writings which are heavily influenced by her, expressions of the same distinctive mode of thought. So how was Mill able to escape to his more customary, moderate, and complex way of thinking? Himmelfarb herself is at pains to show that Harriet held strong views on many issues, and Mill, on her account, willingly, and indeed obsequiously, gave in to her on many points of disagreement. Himmelfarb also quotes from Mill's *Autobiography* on the influence of Harriet in the writing of *The Subjection of Women*. It was through her teaching that Mill became aware of the way in which 'the consequences of the inferior position of women intertwine themselves with all the evils of existing society and with all the difficulties of human improvement'.[40] But this shows Mill's consciousness of the connection between his plea for the equality of the sexes and many other social and political issues which interest him. If therefore it was the liberation of women which led him to adopt Harriet's mode of thought in *On Liberty*, then he had reason also to stick to that mode of thought when he was dealing with other subjects impinging on the liberation of women.

Himmelfarb's second explanation of *On Liberty's* special position is that it was written during the period of Mill's marriage to Harriet when the cause of women dominated his thought more profoundly than at other times. But some of the works of the other Mill were also written or revised during the same period. If the cause of women was in the forefront of his thought when he wrote *On Liberty,* it should, by the same token, also be his dominant interest when he was writing other works at the time.

But assuming that there are indeed two Mills, and setting aside the problem of when and where each Mill expressed himself, how plausible is Himmelfarb's explanation of the driving force behind *On Liberty?* If, as she insists, Mill's purpose in writing *On Liberty* was to promote the cause of women, then why is it that the emancipation of women features only fleetingly in the essay? She speculates that Mill had hoped that by using safer examples, such as religion, he would win support for the general proposition of liberty, and after that, 'all the particulars, including women, would fall into place.'[41] However, this does not explain why, in his letter to Harriet of 15 January 1855, in which he stated the urgency of writing and publishing the essay, there was no reference to the cause of women, but only a reference to the necessity of combating illiberal tendencies.

On my way here cogitating theron I came back to an idea we have talked about and thought that the best thing to write and publish at present would be a volume on Liberty. So many things might be brought into it and nothing seems to be more needed — it is a growing need too, for opinion tends to encroach more and more on liberty, and almost all the projects of social reformers in these days are really *liberticide* — Comte, particularly so.[42]

Several things are evident from this letter. First, it was Mill, and not Harriet, who first drew attention to the urgency of publishing *On Liberty.* Secondly, there was no single issue, like the cause of women, which led him to the belief in the importance of the essay. Himmelfarb's search for a single issue is therefore misguided. The liberation of women may have been too delicate an issue for Mill to write directly and at length about in a published essay. But if, as Himmelfarb claims, 'On Liberty was the case of women writ large',[43] then one would at least expect Mill to mention it in his private communication to his wife. So at the most the cause of women is only one of the 'many things' that the essay is concerned with.

I have argued in Chapter 2 that Mill wanted to revise the whole framework within which the question of individual liberty was discussed, and to make the case for liberty on the 'higher ground of principle'. It was only in the area of religion that this higher ground was acknowledged to some extent, and this is why he picked on religious examples. Mill wanted to show that a principled defence of individual liberty involved its extension from the religious to other areas as well. Himmelfarb's failure to understand the nature of Mill's case for liberty is manifest in her argument that Mill did not write *On Liberty* to defend 'the more serious forms of social and sexual deviancy' because he had 'no great liking' for them.[44] But what Mill liked or disliked is irrelevant, for Mill wrote *On Liberty* precisely to combat the view that the limits of individual liberty should be determined by the 'likings or dislikings of society, or of some powerful portion of it'.

I conclude that although Himmelfarb's emphasis on Mill's continued interest in the emancipation of women, and her story of Harriet's influence on him, are most interesting, she fails in her attempt to weave these fascinating accounts into her general thesis of the two Mills.

But what about the textual evidence drawn from the period before Mill came under Harriet's deep influence? Does it support Himmelfarb's view of the other Mill? I find the same difficulty with the two reviews of de Tocqueville, and with the essay on *Reorganization of the Reform Party*, as I did with some of the essays in the post-Harriet period. Again, I do not doubt that they show Mill to be an imperfect Radical; and if this is all that Himmelfarb wants to establish, then it would be impossible to disagree with her. But if her case is that anyone who is not a perfect Radical violates the letter or the spirit of *On Liberty*, then I fail to follow her. To plead for the gradual instead of the immediate introduction of universal suffrage is not necessarily to violate anything of importance in the essay *On Liberty*. In the second review of Tocqueville, Mill in fact displays the same concern he was to show in the essay *On Liberty* with the provision of opportunities for the expression of individuality, and for the propagation of opinions opposed to those generally held in a society. There is also the fear that the majority may impose its wishes through coercive measures outside the framework of the law.[45]

In her book, Himmelfarb acknowledges some similarities between the themes of the essays on de Tocqueville and those of *On Liberty*.[46] But she argues that Mill attacked the qualities of the commercial class even though these were the very qualities he celebrated in *On Liberty*.[47] Thus, whereas in *On Liberty* Mill regarded 'freedom and variety of situations' as necessary for the promotion of individuality, in the second review of Tocqueville he valued the absence of the commercial spirit among the agricultural class. Unlike the commercial class, farmers in England still had strong attachments to places and persons, and to traditional ways of life. Himmelfarb seems to think that Mill's notion of individuality implies 'freedom from all ties', and that therefore only the commercial spirit is a true expression of it. But Mill pleaded for 'freedom and variety of situations' in order that different individuals might develop in different ways. No doubt some would exercise their freedom by freeing themselves from previous attachments, whereas others would want to cling to them. In the second review of Tocqueville, Mill was fearful of the complete dominance of the commercial spirit because, 'whenever any variety of human nature becomes predominant in a community, it imposes upon all the rest of society its own type; forcing all either to submit to it or to imitate it.'[48] He praised the commercial spirit as 'one of the greatest instruments not only of civilization in the narrowest, but of improvement and culture in the widest sense'.[49] But the agricultural class was still necessary as a counterbalance to the predominance of this spirit. The predominance of any one class or spirit was undesirable because, 'The unlikeness of one man to another is not only a principle of improvement, but would seem almost to be the only principle.'[50]

Mill made alterations to the original versions of the essays on *Bentham* and *Coleridge* when editing *Dissertations and Discussions*, but the alterations in *Bentham* do not seem to bear on the issue of individual liberty. Indeed the fear that individual liberty would be suppressed by the 'despotism of Public Opinion' is as strong here as in the essay *On Liberty*. However, in the essay on *Coleridge* there are some remarks to which Himmelfarb attaches significance.[51] The most important of these for our purposes are concentrated in a passage where Mill is discussing the second of his three essential conditions of all permanent political societies. Himmelfarb lists them among the examples of the more flagrant changes made by Mill which altered the sense and tone of the original.[52] In *Dissertations and Discussions* Mill's changes seem to be designed to underline his belief in freedom much more than was suggested in the original version. There are undoubtedly some important differences in the two versions, but the really crucial question is whether the original version is inconsistent with the acceptance of the principle of individual freedom. Taken in itself, the original version seems to be susceptible *both* of an interpretation which would make it an illiberal doctrine, and of one which makes it clearly liberal.[53] The belief that it is an essential condition of the stability of a society that there should be something which should be settled and not to be called in question could, if narrowly interpreted, set severe restrictions on individual freedom of opinion and action. But, on the other hand, it could also be interpreted more widely to include the principle of individual freedom itself as a factor which stabilizes a society. In the later version of the passage in question Mill in fact adopts the wider interpretation. In his biography of Mill, Bain refers precisely to this passage and writes: 'Grote never ceased to convert this remark into an expression for the standing intolerance of society towards unpopular opinions'.[54] But Bain apparently gave it a different interpretation.

Even in the original version of the essay Mill says that the feeling that there should be something which is not to be called in question 'may attach itself to laws; to ancient liberties, or ordinances; to the whole or some part of the political, or even the domestic, institutions of the state'. With regard to laws which restrain the individual's inclinations to cause harm to others, like the laws against murder and assault, it is surely not illiberal to maintain that unless there is a general recognition that they are right and not to be done away with, there can be no peace and security in a society. Apart from these, Mill's account of the essential conditions of stability in a society need not imply that there would be other specific laws and institutions which should remain unchanged. He may mean no more than that respect for law and ordered government in general should remain unchanged, and not the respect for this or that law or government. Men may seek to change particular laws and institutions by constitutional processes, but they should not disregard and refuse to obey any law they find unacceptable. In seeking to rid society of particular institutions, they should be conscious of the possible cohesive effects of some of these institutions. That something like this is what Mill really meant can be shown if one looks at the passage in question, not in isolation, but in the wider context of the essay as a whole. I have already done this in Chapter 6, and here it is only necessary to summarize some of the relevant points. The essay was written for Radicals and Liberals. He thus sought to emphasize those elements of what he called 'the Germano-Coleridgian school' from which he felt they had most to learn. One of the important problems which this school of thought saw was how to achieve improvement in society while preserving the conditions of social stability. Mill's intention in putting forward the essential conditions for the stability of political societies was not to set severe restraints on freedom of discussion and individual liberty, but to warn reformers to be cautious, and to be sensitive to whatever important values may still reside in old institutions and beliefs, and not to destroy everything regarded as bad without at the same time being able to replace them with something better.

Other passages in the essay on *Coleridge* show that Mill was aware of the importance of individual liberty and freedom of opinion. Thus he writes:

All who are on a level with their age now readily admit that government

ought not to *interdict* men from publishing their opinions, pursuing
their employments, or buying and selling their goods, in whatever
place or manner they deem the most advantageous. Beyond suppressing
force and fraud, governments can seldom, without doing more harm
than good, attempt to chain up the free agency of individuals.[55]

And later he speaks of 'unrestricted freedom of thought'
as the very foremost condition of philosophy.[56]

The essay on *Civilization* (1836), which is also included in
Himmelfarb's collection, shows Mill to be firmly committed
to freedom of inquiry. He argues that the purpose of education is not to impose any particular dogma on individuals,
but to teach and equip them 'to seek the truth, ardently,
vigorously, and disinterestedly'. Once they have been given
the necessary instruments for this search, they should be left
to 'the unshackled use of them'.[57] A university teacher is
not obliged to teach the accepted truths of a society. The
test of his suitability is whether he knows all creeds, and
whether in putting foward his own views he 'states the
arguments for all conflicting opinions fairly'.

In this spirit it is that all the great subjects are taught from the chairs in
German and French Universities. The most distinguished teacher is
selected, whatever be his particular views, and he consequently teaches
in the spirit of free inquiry, not of dogmatic imposition. Were such the
practice here, we believe that the results would greatly eclipse France
and Germany, because we believe that when the restraints on free
speculation and free teaching were taken off, there would be found
in many individual minds among us, a vein of solid and accurate
thought, . . .[58]

The essay therefore gives no indication of illiberal views or
tendencies.

In this essay, as Himmelfarb points out, Mill laments the
fact that there are too many poorly written books. But he
does not argue, as Himmelfarb seems to suggest, that freedom of discussion is the cause of the proliferation of bad
books, nor does he believe that the remedy is to be found in
restricting such freedom. The source of the trouble was that,
'almost every person who can spell, can and will write'.[59]
Mill suggests two remedies. First, there should be co-operation among individuals, and especially among the 'leading
intellects', to provide better guidance to the general public

in distinguishing between good and bad books. Himmelfarb seems to think that an appeal to co-operation goes against the discussion and competition which *On Liberty* seeks to stimulate.[60] But surely Mill intended the co-operating intellects to discuss vigorously the competing ideas in various books before they issued their verdict. Nor is there any suggestion that the general public should merely accept, and never discuss, the choices and recommendations of their guides. Indeed Mill's second remedy is a proper education, which, as we have just seen, will inculcate a desire for truth and a spirit of free inquiry.

Himmelfarb argues that, unlike *On Liberty*, the main idea of the early essays was a denial of any 'single truth'.[61] But the conflict here is only apparent. The 'single truth' that Mill asserted in the essay *On Liberty* is the importance of individual freedom. One reason for his advocacy of freedom of expression is his belief that the truth on specific issues is likely to be complex, many-sided, and shared by more than one system of thought. The acceptance of the 'single truth' of the importance of individual liberty is therefore not only compatible with the belief that on specific problems no single system of thought has the monopoly of truth, but it is also in part supported by that belief.

Himmelfarb also contrasts the 'absolute' nature of Mill's defence of liberty with the moderate and complex mode of thought of the other Mill. In Chapter 2 I have tried to elucidate the sense in which Mill's liberty principle is 'absolute'. But it is important to notice here that Himmelfarb robs Mill's principle of whatever plausibility it has by ignoring the limited scope of its application.[62] The principle is to be applied to cases in which the state or society interferes with the individual's conduct simply to enforce the values of a dominant or any other group, or to prevent the individual from harming himself. Mill's principle condemns such interference, and seeks to restrict intervention to cases where there is the prevention of harm to others. But Himmelfarb converts this principle to cover 'the entire range of action',[63] and she makes liberty into Mill's 'only value'.[64] She is thereby able to claim that the Mill of *On Liberty*, unlike the other Mill, did not qualify and supplement liberty with other values like 'duty, morality, discipline, the public good, tradition, community, nationality, society'.[65] With this caricature of the liberal Mill it is not surprising that she finds evidence of the other Mill all over Mill's other works. Thus she asserts that *On Liberty* is a rejection of 'community, fraternity and morality'.[66] On the other hand, she points out that in *Utlitarianism* Mill refers to the development of morality by means of sanctions or punishment.[67] But she does not show that Mill believed in using punishment for any other purpose than to prevent harm to others, and this surely is the crucial point if there is to be any contrast between the two works. Again, she picks out Mill's reference in the essay on *Coleridge* to the need for 'restraining discipline' as further evidence of the other Mill.[68] But she fails to notice Mill's remark in *On Liberty:* 'To be held to rigid rules of justice for the sake of others, develops the feelings and capacities which have the good of others for their object.'[69] The question to which *On Liberty* addresses itself is not whether there should be sanctions, punishment, or restraints, but where they are to be applied.

Himmelfarb also treats Mill's doctrine of individuality as if it were a plea for selfishness and self-indulgence,[70] when in fact Mill in *On Liberty* is quite explicit that individuality should be developed 'within the limits imposed by the rights and interests of others',[71] and he pleads for 'a great increase of disinterested exertion to promote the good of others'.[72]

IV. THE YOUNG MILL

The only essay in Himmelfarb's collection which gives some support to her thesis about the two Mills is *The Spirit of the Age*. This consists of a series of articles published in the *Examiner* from 9 January to 29 May 1831. The essay shows a Mill whose views on individual liberty differ from those expressed in *On Liberty* and elsewhere, though the exact differences are of great interest and merit close attention. Packe has also drawn attention to Mill's letter to Sterling of 20 to 22 October 1831 which, according to him, shows Mill to be a 'stern authoritarian'.[73] Packe, however, regards this as a brief aberration which vanished less than eighteen months later with the publication of *On Genius*.

What exactly are Mill's views during this period — 1831 and thereabouts? Even in this 'sternly authoritarian' frame of mind, Mill did not deny the importance of freedom of discussion. In *The Spirit of the Age* he says that an increase in discussion causes the decay of prejudices, and leads to the rooting out of errors. 'It is', he adds, 'by discussion, also, that true opinions are discovered and diffused', though 'this is not so certain a consequence as the weakening of error.'[74] The truth is many-sided, and men are inclined to see only one side of it. But there is no suggestion here that the solution lies in the restriction of freedom of discussion. So too, in his letter to Sterling, Mill writes:

In the Present age of transition, everything must be subordinate to *freedom of inquiry*: if your opinion, or mine, are right, they will in time be unanimously adopted by the instructed classes, and *then* it will be time to found the national creed upon the assumption of their truth.[75]

Himmelfarb, however, quotes from a letter to Carlyle of 18 May 1833, which at first sight seems to indicate that Mill did not care much for freedom of discussion. But a careful examination of the letter does not, I think, bear this out. The relevant part reads:

... it seems to me that there has been on my part something like a want of courage in avoiding, or touching only perfunctorily, with you, points on which I thought it likely that we should differ. That was a kind of reaction from the dogmatic disputatiousness of my former narrow and mechanical state. I have not any great notion of the advantage of what the 'free discussion' men call the 'collision of opinions', it being my creed that Truth is *sown* and germinates in the mind itself, and is not to be struck *out* suddenly like fire from a flint by knocking another hard body against it: so I accustomed myself to *learn* by inducing others to deliver their thoughts, and to teach by scattering my own, and I eschewed occasions of controversy (except occasionally with some of my old Utilitarian associates).[76]

Mill was not against freedom of discussion in the sense of allowing the propagation of different and hostile opinions. Indeed he speaks of learning from the thoughts of others. But he was against 'dogmatic disputatiousness', a frame of mind which revels in criticizing and attacking the doctrines of others, while at the same time being unwilling to seek the element of truth in these doctrines. His reasons for opposition to 'dogmatic disputatiousness' are stated at greater length in a letter to D'Eichthal of 9 February 1830, where he explains that if controversy were avoided,

> no one's offended *amour propre* would make him cling to his errors; no one would connect, with the adoption of truth, the idea of defeat; and no one would feel impelled by the ardour of debate and the desire of triumph, to reject, as almost all now do whatever of truth there really is in the opinions of those whose ultimate conclusion differs from theirs.[77]

What is, however, somewhat confusing is the fact that Mill sometimes says that he is against 'discussion' when what he is really against is disputatiousness. Thus he tells D'Eichthal that he would read all the literature he gets about the Saint-Simonian doctrines, ask for any necessary explanations, and always state his reasons for differing from these doctrines; but, he adds, 'on no account will I discuss with you.'[78] Mill's present dislike of controversy is a reaction against the zeal with which he rushed into disputes at the London Debating Society. Sterling's withdrawal from that Society after his debate with Mill may have hastened and sustained this reaction. But Mill did not reject the importance of freedom of discussion. He merely recognized that injured pride and other human frailties may obstruct the acquisition of true opinions. Even the Mill of *On Liberty*, the staunch defender of freedom of discussion, was fully aware that men, engaged in strong controversies, might refuse to see the truth:

> I acknowledge that the tendency of all opinions to become sectarian is not cured by the freest discussion, but is often heightened and exacerbated thereby; the truth which ought to have been, but was not, seen, being rejected all the more violently because proclaimed by persons regarded as opponents. But it is not on the impassioned partisan, it is on the calmer and more disinterested bystander, that this collision of opinions works its salutary effect.[79]

In the case of his private letters there were of course no disinterested bystanders to profit from any controversy. But Mill had faith in the value of an exchange of views, for in a letter of 20 October 1832 he speaks of the good of 'association & collision with other minds'.[80]

But though the evidence does not show that the Mill of

this period was against freedom of discussion, it does show that there is a significant difference between Mill's views in *The Spirit of the Age* and those in *On Liberty*. It lies in his evaluation of the value of freedom of discussion for the ordinary man. In the essay *On Liberty* Mill thinks that freedom of thought is indispensable 'to enable average human beings to attain the mental stature which they are capable of'.[81] Freedom of discussion is needed so that men may not only have true opinions, but that they may also *know* the truth. To know the truth one has to know the grounds for it, and be prepared to listen to conflicting views, and modify one's own view in the light of further argument and evidence; it is not enough merely to accept an opinion and believe in it on trust or blindly. In the presence of freedom of discussion 'even persons of the most ordinary intellect' may be raised to 'something of the dignity of thinking beings'.[82] But in *The Spirit of the Age* and in the letter to Sterling (20 to 22 October 1832), Mill held a different view. He did not believe that the ordinary man had sufficient opportunities for acquiring the knowledge or experience which would enable him to *know* the truth. He must in the end always accept his opinions on trust from those who have devoted themselves specially to the study of moral and political philosophy. Freedom of discussion was valued because it enabled ordinary men to have true opinions and not because it enabled them to know the truth. To know the truth was the privilege of the more cultivated men.[83]

But even at this period of his life Mill believed that the ordinary man should not be forced to accept the unanimous opinions of the more cultivated minds. In his description of the natural state of society, he says that the opinions and feelings of the people are to be formed for them 'with their voluntary acquiescence'.[84] On the other hand, he wanted society to be so organized that 'wordly power' was put in the hands of the more cultivated members so as 'to render their power over the minds of their fellow-citizens paramount and irresistible'.[85] In this effort to make the power of the cultivated minds 'irresistible', in the apparent lack of any concern over the possible 'spiritual and temporal despotism' such a power might exercise, and in his omission to define any area of a man's life except that of his own 'particular calling or occupation' where he is capable of *knowing* the truth, the Mill of this period differed radically from the Mill of *On Liberty* and also of *Auguste Comte and Positivism*.

However, when the essay *On Genius* was published in October 1832, Mill had already discarded some elements in his doctrine that the people should accept their ideas on the authority of the more cultivated minds. This essay is a strong plea that it is the duty of *all* men to seek to *know* the truth in certain areas and that they should not be satisfied with accepting it on trust:

> Let each person be made to feel that in other things he may believe upon trust — if he find a trustworthy authority — but that in the line of his peculiar duty, and in the line of the duties common to all men, it is his business to *know*.[86] *(Mill's italics.)*

The ideal of knowing the truth, of the desirability of the 'active' as opposed to the 'passive' mind, so prominent in the essay *On Liberty*, was already dominating Mill's thoughts here. And here too, as in *On Liberty*, it was an ideal that he held out for all men, and not just for a few limited number of cultivated ones.[87]

It is difficult to ascertain when exactly Mill changed his views. Himmelfarb seems to think that there is a continuity of beliefs between *The Spirit of the Age* and a second series of articles which Mill wrote for the *Examiner* in 1832 and which lost the paper about two hundred Radical readers. If this is correct, then the essay *On Genius* is probably the first expression of his changed views. However, I do not think that Himmelfarb is correct about the articles she mentions. These are two articles on pledges published on 1 and 15 July 1832. Mill contended there that, except for a few cases, no pledges should be exacted from intending Members of Parliament. However, his arguments show that while he believed that legislation should be in the hands of the more cultivated minds, he was none the less alive to the dangers of unchecked power, even if exercised by wise men. He felt that legislation, like medicine, is a profession, and that if legislators were chosen on the basis of their greater political wisdom, it would then be ridiculous for the electors to impose their own views on them through the pledge. But he regarded the people's right of periodically changing their legislators as a security against the abuse of power by the legislators:

Government must be performed by the few, for the benefit of the many: and the security of the many consists in being governed by those who possess the largest share of their confidence, and no longer than while that confidence lasts.[88]

To strengthen this security, Mill advocated a shortening of the duration of parliaments. He feared the corruption of continued power. There is here no overemphasis on the good which a group of cultivated intellects may produce. Here is a Mill conscious of the need for checks even on the power of this group. Mill always retained a respect for the leadership of the cultivated minds, but the extreme confidence in their 'irresistible power' does not seem to have lived beyond 1831.

What about the Mill of the 1820s? In *Prefaces to Liberty*,[89] Bernard Wishy has conveniently brought together a number of Mill's writings on liberty leading up to the essay *On Liberty*. Many of these belong to the period 1823 to 1828, and we see the young Mill ardently defending individual freedom against religious persecution, and arguing for freedom of discussion. Of special interest is an article on religious persecutions from *The Westminister Review* of July 1824, and another article on the liberty of the press and the law of libel published in April 1825. Mill argues that persecution may force the unbeliever to conform outwardly to the requirements of the accepted religious system, but it cannot ensure a genuine and sincere change of mind. Christians are reminded that their religion breathes 'charity, liberty, and mercy, in every line', and that it is 'monstrous' for them to use their power to crush and persecute others in the same way as they themselves have been persecuted when they were not in power.[90] In arguments similar to those in *On Liberty* about the desirability of freedom of discussion both when the received opinion is false or partly false, as well as when it is true, Mill warns that 'religion divorced from reason will sink into a mere prejudice, losing the power of truth as the proofs of its truth are unregarded, and becoming feeble for resistance and worthless in its influence',[91] and maintains that even when the existing religion of a country is already absolutely perfect, freedom of discussion should be welcome because it leads to 'a more general and vivid perception' of the value of the religion, and thus strengthens and extends its influence.[92] To the argument that the people are ignorant and incapable of forming true opinions, Mill replies that it is only through discussion that their ignorance can be removed. The suppression of discussion is the cause of ignorance, and freedom of discussion is the cure. Freedom of discussion also acts as a check on the abuse of power.[93]

But Wishy is right to point out that at this period Mill was more sanguine about 'the disinterestedness of public opinion' than later on in his life.[94] Mill at this stage regarded public opinion as a great check on any interference with individual liberty. He was later to accuse Bentham of 'rivetting the yoke of public opinion closer and closer round the necks of all public functionaries, and excluding every possibility of the exercise of the slightest or most temporary influence either by a minority, or by the functionary's own notions of right'.[95] But in the 1820s there was no talk of 'the despotism of Public Opinion', only of its liberating influence. This belief in the effectiveness of public opinion in preventing the corruptions of power reached its climax in the Speech on Perfectibility delivered to the London Debating Society in 1828 in which Mill concludes:

And there is another thing that is requisite: to take men out of the sphere of the opinion of their separate and private coteries and make them amenable to the general tribunal of the public at large; to leave no class possessed of power sufficient to protect one another in defying public opinion, and to manufacture a separate code of morality for their private guidance; and so to organize the political institutions of a country that no one could possess any power save what might be given to him by the favourable sentiments, not of any separate class with a separate interest, but of the people.[96]

Mill's change of mind was a gradual affair. In the *Autobiography* he describes his mental crisis of 1826 when he became disillusioned with his Benthamite beliefs, but it was only in 1829 that he first came into contact with Saint-Simonian doctrines, the influence of which is so conspicuous in *The Spirit of the Age*. In that year he had already accepted the necessity of a *Pouvoir Spirituel*,[97] though he was still much less sympathetic to these doctrines than he was to be in 1831.

There are, then, three phases in the development of Mill's views on liberty. In the earliest phase of the 1820s, he was fearful of any power that might be exercised without the control of public opinion. Then in *The Spirit of the Age* he seems to have advocated a passive acceptance by the public of the enlightened doctrines propounded by more cultivated minds. From a belief in 'the disinterestedness of public opinion' he swung over to a belief in the disinterestedness of the opinions of cultivated minds. Finally, in what is by far the longest phase, his fear of 'the tyranny of the majority' was tempered by a realization that even wise men are capable of being corrupted, and by an increasing belief in the importance of the free, spontaneous, and active development of all men. This third phase culminated, of course, in the essay *On Liberty*, where the leadership of the more cultivated minds, and their constant challenges to established and customary beliefs, are accepted as very valuable, but at the same time the chief justification of freedom of discussion is seen as consisting of the opportunities it provides for the flowering of 'an intellectually active people'. In none of these phases did Mill reject freedom of discussion. The cause of individual freedom was Mill's lifelong preoccupation. His analysis of the threats to freedom, and the barriers he believed should be erected against them, varied from time to time. But they were problems which were never far from his thoughts. It is as the passionate champion of individual liberty that he has been, and generally still is, attacked or admired. As parts of the essay *On Liberty*, which appear to be ambiguous, are illuminated by other works of his, our understanding of him will no doubt increase. But by reading too much into some of his statements, and by focusing attention on one aspect of his thought or life at the expense of the rest, one may be tempted to reject, or radically modify, the traditional picture of him as the great liberal. That would be a grave error.

Notes

1. INTRODUCTION

1. *On Liberty* in *Utilitarianism, Liberty, Representative Government* (Everyman edn). All subsequent references to *On Liberty* and *Utilitarianism* are to this edition.
2. Wilmore Kendall, 'The "Open Society" and Its Fallacies', in Peter Radcliff (ed.), *Limits of Liberty: Studies of Mill's On Liberty* (Belmont, 1966).
3. Robert Paul Wolff *The Poverty of Liberalism* (Boston, 1969).
4. *On Liberty*, p. 74. The Everyman edition reads 'of a man' and not 'of man'. But the latter reading appears in the fourth and final Library Edition (1869) in Mill's lifetime. The former reading appears in the People's Edition (1865). Cf. John M. Robson, 'Textual Introduction', *Essays on Politics and Society: Collected Works of John Stuart Mill*, Vol. xvii (Toronto & London, 1977), pp. lxxxiv–v, fn. 37. Using the reading in the People's Edition, some commentators have attached significance to the indefinite article. Cf. John Rawls, *A Theory of Justice* (Oxford, 1972), p. 209 fn. 7; and J. L. Mackie, 'Can there be a Right-Based Moral Theory?', *Midwest Studies in Philosophy*, iii (1978), p. 355.
5. See: J. L. Mackie, *Ethics: Inventing Right and Wrong* (Penguin, 1977), Ch. 6. Jonathan Glover, *Causing Death and Saving Lives* (Penguin, 1977), pp. 62–6; and J. J. C. Smart, 'Hedonistic and Ideal Utilitarianism', *Midwest Studies in Philosophy*, iii (1978). Smart refers to 'satisfaction utlitiarianism' instead of 'preference utilitarianism'. For useful discussions of utilitarianism in general see: J. J. C. Smart and Bernard Williams, *Utilitarianism: For and Against* (Cambridge, 1973); and Dan W. Brock, 'Recent Work in Utilitarianism', *American Philosophical* Quarterly, 10 (1973). A useful collection of essays on utilitarianism with particular reference to Mill is S. Gorovitz (ed.), *Mill: Utilitarianism, with Critical Essays* (Indianapolis, 1971).
6. The differences and similarities between classical utilitarianism and preference utilitarianism are discussed further in Ch. 4.
7. This point is discussed further in Chs. 2 and 4.

2. SELF-REGARDING CONDUCT

1. This kind of objection to Mill has been well documented and discussed by J. C. Rees. See: 'A Re-Reading of Mill on Liberty', *Political Studies*, viii (1960), repr. with new postcript, in Peter Radcliff (ed.), *Limits of Liberty: Studies of Mill's On Liberty* (Belmont, 1966); 'Individualism and Individual Liberty', *Il Politico*, 26 (1961); and *Mill and his Early Critics* (Leicester, 1956), pp. 35–8.
2. Robert Paul Wolff, *The Poverty of Liberalism* (Boston, 1969), p. 24.
3. John Morley, 'Mr. Mill's Doctrine of Liberty', *Fortnightly Review* (1 August 1873), p. 252.
4. Ibid., p. 253.
5. Op. cit. Subsequent references to this paper will be to the Radcliff edn.
6. Ibid., p. 94.

7. Richard Wollheim, 'John Stuart Mill and the Limits of State Action', *Social Research*, 40 (1973), p. 6.

8. Ted Honderich, *Punishment, the Supposed Justifications* (London, 1969), Ch. 6, esp. pp. 181–6.

9. Cf. Richard Wollheim, 'John Stuart Mill and the Limits of State Action', op. cit., pp. 22–4.

10. Rees draws attention to this passage and acknowledges that Mill is here conceding that self-regarding conduct can affect the interests of others, though not 'directly' or 'primarily'. However, he thinks that to explore these distinctions would be to make Mill's principle extremely complicated, contrary to Mill's remark that his principle is 'very simple'. Cf. 'A Re-Reading of Mill on Liberty', op. cit., p. 100.

11. *Utilitarianism*, p. 13.

12. Ibid., pp. 13–14.

13. Op. cit. All subsequent references to Wollheim in this section are to this paper. Wollheim's latest paper on Mill is 'John Stuart Mill and Isaiah Berlin: The Ends of Life and the Preliminaries of Morality', in Alan Ryan (ed.), *The Idea of Freedom: Essays in Honour of Isaiah Berlin* (Oxford, 1979). Wollheim explains 'the complex character of Mill's commitment to utilitarianism', but there is no further detailed discussion of Mill's defence of liberty.

14. John Rawls, *A Theory of Justice* (Oxford, 1972), p. 450.

15. J. B. Schneewind (ed.), *Mill's Ethical Writings* (New York and London, 1965), p. 274.

16. Cf. J. B. Schneewind (ed.), *Mill's Essays on Literature and Society* (New York and London, 1965), p. 284

17. See Wollheim, p. 22.

18. Cf. Joel Feinberg, ' "Harmless Immoralities" and Offensive Nuisances', in Norman S. Care and Thomas K. Trelogan (eds.), *Issues in Law and Morality* (Cleveland and London, 1973), pp. 104–5.

19. See J. J. C. Smart, 'Extreme and Restricted Utilitarianism', in Samuel Gorovitz (ed.), *Mill: Utilitarianism, with Critical Essays* (Indianapolis, 1971), pp. 197–8.

20. Ronald Dworkin, *Taking Rights Seriously* (London, 1978), p. 236.

21. Ibid., pp. 234, 275. Brian Barry makes a similar distinction between privately-oriented and publicly-oriented judgements and wants. Cf. *Political Argument* (London, 1965), pp. 12–13, 62–6, 71–2, 142–3, 295–9.

22. Ibid., p. 358.

23. Ibid., pp. 235, 275.

24. Ibid., p. 235.

25. Cf. Joseph Raz, 'Professor Dworkin's Theory of Rights', *Political Studies*, 26 (1978), p. 131; and H. L. A. Hart, 'Between Utility and Rights', in Alan Ryan (ed.), *The Idea of Freedom : Essays in Honour of Isaiah Berlin* (Oxford, 1979), pp. 91–3. Both papers make many other acute criticisms of Dworkin's arguments.

26. See Hart's comments on this in 'Between Utility and Rights', ibid., pp. 93–7.

27. Cf. Bernard Williams, 'A critique of utilitarianism', in J. J. C. Smart and Bernard Williams, *Utilitarianism: For and Against* (Cambridge, 1973). p. 112.

28. *Taking Rights Seriously*, p. 236.

29. Rolf E. Sartorius, *Individual Conduct and Social Norms* (Belmont, 1975), Ch. 8, Sect. 3. See also David Lyons, 'Human Rights and the General Welfare', *Philosophy and Public Affairs*, 6 (1977).

30. Ibid., p. 157.

31. Ibid., pp. 160–1.

32. *On Liberty*, p. 142.
33. James Fitzjames Stephen, *Liberty, Equality, Fraternity*, ed. with introduction and notes by R. J. White (Cambridge, 1967).
34. Leslie Stephen, *The Life of Sir James Ftizjames Stephen* (London, 1895), p. 308.
35. Leslie Stephen, *The English Utilitarians, Vol. iii: John Stuart Mill* (London, 1900), p. 244 fn 1.
36. *Principles of Morals and Legislation*, Ch. v, Sect. xi.
37. *Liberty, Equality, Fraternity*, op. cit., p. 162.
38. Ibid., p. 157.
39. Hart draws attention to this argument in *Law, Liberty and Morality* (London, 1963), pp. 60—9.
40. *A History of the Criminal Law of England*, Vol. ii (London, 1883), p. 82.
41. R. M. Hare, 'Ethical Theory and Utilitarianism', in H. D. Lewis (ed.), *Contemporary British Philosophy: Personal Statements*, 4th Series (London, 1976). See also J. L. Mackie's comments on this theory in 'Can there be a Right-Based Moral Theory?', *Midwest Studies in Philosophy*, iii (1978), p. 353.
42. Ibid., p. 123.
43. Cf. Ted Honderich, 'The Worth of J. S. Mill *On Liberty*', *Political Studies*, xxii (1974).
44. Patrick Devlin, *The Enforcement of Morals* (London, 1965), p. 110.
45. Ibid., p. 14. I discuss in great detail Devlin's criticisms of Mill in Ch. 6.
46. Cf. H. L. A. Hart, *The Morality of the Criminal Law* (Oxford, 1965), pp. 48—9.

3. MORALITY AND UTILITY

1. See: 'Mr McCloskey on Mill's Liberalism', *The Philosophical Quarterly*, 14 (1964); 'John Stuart Mill's Art of Living', *The Listener*, 21 October 1965; *The Philosophy of John Stuart Mill* (London, 1970); and *John Stuart Mill* (London, 1974).
2. *The Philosophy of John Stuart Mill*, p. 236.
3. Ibid., p. 240.
4. The most valuable of these are the works of D. G. Brown and David Lyons. For Brown's contributions, see: 'Mill on Liberty and Morality', *Philosophical Review*, lxxxi (1972); 'What is Mill's Principle of Utility?', *Canadian Journal of Philosophy*, 3 (1973); and 'Mill on Harm to Others' Interests', *Political Studies*, xxvi (1978). For Lyons's contributions see: 'Mill's Theory of Morality', *Nous*, 10 (1976); 'Human Rights and the General Welfare', *Philosophy and Public Affairs*, 6 (1977); and 'Mill's Theory of Justice' in Alvin I. Goldman and Jaegwon Kim (eds.), *Values and Morals* (Dordrecht, 1978).
5. J. B. Schneewind (ed.), *Mill's Ethical Writings* (New York and London, 1965), p. 165.
6. For a brief and lucid account of Mill's theory, see: John R. Baker, 'Utilitarianism and "Secondary Principles" ', *The Philosophical Quarterly*, 21 (1971).
7. *Mill's Ethical Writings*, Schneewind (ed.), p. 162.
8. Ibid., p. 166.
9. *Utilitarianism*, p. 46. Cited by D. G. Brown, 'Mill on Liberty and Morality', op. cit., p. 154.
10. Cited by Ryan, *The Philosophy of John Stuart Mill*, p. 215.
11. *Mill's Ethical Writings*, Schneewind (ed.), p. 168.
12. 'Mill on Liberty and Morality', op. cit., p. 156 f. See also: 'What is Mill's Principle of Utility?', op. cit.

13. See the papers listed in fn. 4.
14. *Utilitarianism*, p. 45.
15. 'Human Rights and the General Welfare', op. cit., p. 121. Here he differs from the interpretations of Brown and Ryan which stress the connection between morality and the external sanctions.
16. 'Mill's Theory of Morality', op. cit., p. 108; 'Human Rights and the General Welfare', p. 122.
17. 'Mill's Theory of Morality', pp. 118—19.
18. Ibid., p. 117 (Lyons's italics).

4. HARM TO OTHERS

1. Cf. J. R. Lucas, *The Principles of Politics* (Oxford, 1966), pp. 172—5; Ernest Nagel, 'The Enforcement of Morals', in Paul Kurtz (ed.), *Moral Problems in Contemporary Society* (Englewood Cliffs, 1969), pp. 141—7. The following discussions of the concept of harm are relevant to Mill's principle: Joel Feinberg, *Social Philosophy* (New Jersey, 1973), Ch. 2; Richard Taylor, *Freedom, Anarchy, and the Law* (New Jersey, 1973), Chs. ix and x; John Kleinig, 'Crime and the Concept of Harm', *American Philosophical Quarterly*, 15 (1978); and Alan Gewirth, *Reason and Morality* (Chicago and London, 1978), pp. 212—5, 230—6.
2. 'Wrongness and Harm', in R. M. Hare, *Essays on the Moral Concepts* (London, 1972), p. 97.
3. Ibid., p. 98.
4. Ibid., p. 102.
5. Hare refers to the harming of the dying man's interests in 'Ethical Theory and Utilitarianism', H. D. Lewis (ed.), *Contemporary British Philosophy: Personal Statements*, pp. 130—1. See also, Joel Feinberg, 'Harm and Self-Interest', in P. M. S. Hacker and J. Raz (eds.), *Law, Morality, and Society: Essays in Honour of H. L. A. Hart* (Oxford, 1977) p. 302.
6. 'Reply to "Liberals, Fanatics and Not-so-innocent-Bystanders" ', in B. Y Khanbhai, R. S. Katz, and R. A. Pineau (eds.), *Jowett Papers* (1968—9), p. 52.
7. *On Liberty*, p. 75.
8. Ibid., p. 132.
9. Ibid., p. 136.
10. H. L. A. Hart, *The Concept of Law* (Oxford, 1961), pp. 189—95.
11. Ibid., p. 188.
12. See: Basil Mitchell, *Law, Morality and Religion in a Secular Society* (London, 1967) and 'Law and the Protection of Institutions', in *The Proper Study*, Royal Institute of Philosophy Lectures, Vol. 4 (1969—70).
13. This is discussed in Chs. 6 and 9.
14. *On Liberty*, p. 150.
15. Ibid., p. 121.
16. Hart points out that recognition of the minimum content of natural law does not imply that the rules are fair and morally acceptable. Cf. *The Concept of Law*, pp. 195—6.
17. See *On Liberty*, pp. 73—4.
18. 'Mill on Liberty and Morality', *Philosophical Review*, lxxxi (1972), p. 145.
19. But even this broader formulation does not satisfy Brown who thinks that it does not cover the failure to bear one's fair share in the joint work necessary to the interest of society. But perhaps Brown interprets this rather broadly. Mill limits the 'fair share' to actions within the social domain.

20. H. J. McCloskey, *John Stuart Mill: A Critical Study* (London, 1971), p. 108.

21. John Harris, 'The Survival Lottery', *Philosophy*, 50 (1975).
22. Cf. Peter Singer, 'Utility and the Survival Lottery', *Philosophy*, 52 (1977).
23. *On Liberty*, p. 132.
24. 'Use and Abuse of Political Terms', *Essays on Politics and Society, Collected Works of John Stuart Mill*, Vol. xvii (Toronto and London, 1977), p. 11.
25. But see G. L. Williams, 'Mill's Principle of Liberty', *Political Studies*, xxiv (1976).
26. 'Mill on Harm to Others' Interests', *Political Studies*, xxvi (1978), pp. 397—8.
27. Cf. J. R. Lucas, *The Principles of Politics*, p. 174; and Ernest Nagel, 'The Enforcement of Morals', op. cit.
28. *On Liberty*, p. 28.
29. Ibid., p. 74.

5. INDIVIDUALITY

1. Isaiah Berlin stresses the importance Mill attaches to the freedom to choose. Cf. *John Stuart Mill and the Ends of Life* (London, 1959), repr. in *Four Essays on Liberty* (Oxford, 1979).
2. R. P. Anschutz, *The Philosophy of J. S. Mill* (London, 1963), p. 25.
3. Ibid., p. 27.
4. *Utilitarianism*, p. 7.
5. Bentham's view of liberty is discussed by Douglas Long, *Bentham on Liberty* (Toronto, 1977).
6. Cf. Richard B. Friedman, 'A New Exploration of Mill's Essay On Liberty', *Political Studies*, xiv (1966).
7. 'Freedom and Happiness in Mill's Defence of Liberty', *The Philosophical Quarterly*, 28 (1978).
8. Ibid., p. 331.
9. *Utilitarianism*, p. 47.
10. Bogen and Farrell, p. 334.
11. Ibid., p. 328.
12. Ibid., p. 336.
13. Cf. Bernard Williams, 'A Critique of utilitariansim', in J. J. C. Smart and Bernard Williams, *Utilitariansim: for and against* (Cambridge, 1973), pp. 84—5.
14. Bernard Williams discusses the problem of distinguishing consequentialism from non-consequentialism, ibid., Sect. 2. See also: J. J. C. Smart, 'An outline of a system of utilitarian ethics', in the same volume, p. 41; J. J. C. Smart, 'Hedonistic and Ideal Utilitarianism' in *Midwest Studies in Philosophy*, iii (1978), pp. 245—6, 248—9; and H. J. McCloskey, *John Stuart Mill: A Critical Study* (London, 1971), pp. 71—2. Using Mill as an illustration, J. L. Mackie shows how a 'goal-based' moral theory can change into a 'right-based theory which treats as central 'the right of persons progressively to choose how they shall live'. Cf. 'Can there be a Right-Based Moral Theory?', *Midwest Studies in Philosophy*, iii (1978). The distinctions between goal-based, right-based, and duty-based theories are made by Ronald Dworkin, in *Taking Rights Seriously* (London, 1978), ch 6.
15. Robert F. Ladenson gives a utilitarian account of Mill's defence of individuality. According to him, when Mill says that individuality has 'intrinsic worth', he simply means that people desire individuality as a source of pleasure in its own right. But this does not explain the importance Mill attaches to the intrinsic worth of individuality, for Mill believes that only a few persons desire individuality for this reason. See 'Mill's Conception of Individuality', *Social Theory and Practice*, 4 (1977), p. 169.

16. 'Mill on Pleasure and Self-Development', *The Philosophical Quarterly*, 16 (1966), p. 70.
17. I am indebted to Professor H. L. A. Hart for raising this point with me.
18. *A Theory of Justice* (Oxford, 1972), p. 210.
19. J. D. Mabbott argues that Mill's treatment of liberty as valuable in itself has this implication. Mabbott's argument is quoted and critically discussed by S. I. Benn and R. S. Peters, *Social Principles and the Democratic State* (London, 1959), pp. 200–22, and by Basil Mitchell, *Law, Morality, and Religion in a Secular Society* (London, 1967), pp. 95–7.
20. Ibid., Ch. 6.
21. *Philosophy*, 36 (1961).
22. Mitchell, op. cit., p. 92.
23. Ibid., p. 97.
24. This is only one of his arguments for freedom of discussion. Cf. Ch. 8.
25. Cf. R. S. Downie and Elizabeth Telfer, *Respect for Persons* (London, 1969), pp. 71–6.

6. ENFORCING SHARED VALUES

1. Patrick Devlin, *The Enforcement of Morals* (London, 1965).
2. Cf. H. L. A. Hart, 'Social Solidarity and the Enforcement of Morals', *University of Chicago Law Review*, 35 (1967).
3. Ibid., p. 2. Hart takes this characterization of the conservative thesis from R. Dworkin, 'Lord Devlin and the Enforcement of Morals', *Yale Law Journal*, 75 (1966). Dworkin's paper is reprinted under the title 'Liberty and Moralism', in Ronald Dworkin, *Taking Rights Seriously* (London, 1978), Ch 10.
4. This analogy has been effectively criticized by H. L. A. Hart in 'Immorality and Treason', *The Listener*, 30 July 1959, repr. in Richard A. Wasserstrom (ed.), *Morality and the Law* (Belmont, 1971). See also Joel Feinberg, *Social Philosophy* (New Jersey, 1973), pp. 38–9.
5. Devlin's principles are very similar to Fitzjames Stephen's conditions for determining when the criminal law should be used against immoralities. See, *Liberty, Equality, Fraternity* (Cambridge, 1967), pp. 159–60.
6. Devlin, p. 17.
7. Ibid., p. 133.
8. Ibid., p. 113.
9. Ibid., p. 114.
10. Ibid., p. 112.
11. Ibid., p. 114.
12. But see Hart, 'Social Solidarity and the Enforcement of Morals', op. cit., p. 13.
13. Noel B. Reynolds, 'The Enforcement of Morals and the Rule of Law', *Georgia Law Review*, ii (1977), p. 1335.
14. Devlin. p. 108.
15. *Social Philosophy*, op. cit., pp. 25, 37.
16. Ibid., p. 25.
17. Ibid., p. 37.
18. In 'Individualism and Individual Liberty', *Il Politico*, 26 (1961), J. C. Rees distinguishes between different senses of individualism, and defends Mill against the charge of false individualism. As Rees points out, Mill was alive to the fact that 'so long as individuals retained their power of choice and decision' there is 'the permanent possibility of conflict' between the individual and the society or the state. For a helpful analysis of the different senses of individualism, see also Steven Lukes, *Individualism* (Oxford, 1973).

19. John Stuart Mill, *Autobiography* World's Classics edn., p. 185.
20. I discuss some of these amendments in Ch. 9. The passage is collated in the *Collected Works of John Stuart Mill,* Vol. x (Toronto and London, 1969), Appendix D, pp. 503—8.
21. *Collected Works,* x, p. 134.
22. *Utilitarianism, Liberty and Representative Government* (Everyman edn.), p. 360.
23. *Collected Works,* x, pp. 133—4.
24. *Law, Liberty, and Morality* (London, 1963), p. 70.
25. *Collected Works,* x, p. 134.
26. Ibid., p. 153.
27. Ibid., p. 163.
28. 'Bentham', *Collected Works,* x, p. 79.
29. 'Coleridge', *Collected Works,* x, p. 138.
30. *Representative Government,* p. 189.
31. Cf. P. H. Partridge, *Consent and Consensus* (London, 1971), Chs. 4—6.
32. Ibid., pp. 89 f. Partridge criticizes such theories at pp. 93—5.
33. Cf. Anthony Giddens (ed.), *Emile Durkheim: Selected Writings* (Cambridge, 1972), pp. 141—50 and Giddens's 'Introduction', pp. 3—12. See also Hart, 'Social Solidarity and the Enforcement of Morals', op. cit.
34. Cf. Steven Lukes, *Emile Durkheim, His Life and Work* (London, 1973), pp. 166—7; and idem, 'Durkheim's "Individualism and the Intellectuals" ', *Political Studies,* xvii (1969), which includes a translation of Durkheim's essay. This essay is a powerful corrective to the contrast that Robert Paul Wolff draws between Durkheim and Mill. Cf. *The Poverty of Liberalism* (Boston, 1969), pp. 142—8.
35. *Collected Works,* x, p. 134.
36. Cf. Nicholas Capaldi, 'Censorship and Social Stability in J. S. Mill', *The Mill News Letter,* Vol. ix, No. 1 (1973).
37. *Law, Morality, and Religion in a Secular Society* (London, 1967).
38. Ibid., pp. 31—5.
39. Ibid., p. 67.
40. Ibid., p. 32.
41. Ibid., p. 34.
42. Ibid., p. 34.
43. Ibid., p. 34.
44. Devlin, p. 92.
45. Ibid., p. 96.
46. Ibid., p. 94.
47. Mitchell, p. 25.
48. Ibid., p. 122.
49. *Law, Liberty and Morality,* op. cit., pp. 38—48. Hart's position is criticized by David A. Conway, 'Law, Liberty and Indecency', *Philosophy,* 49 (1974).
50. Joel Feinberg, ' "Harmless Immoralities" and Offensive Nuisances', in Norman S. Care and Thomas K. Trelogan (eds.), *Issues in Law and Morality* (Cleveland and London, 1973). See also the comments by Michael D. Bayles and Feinberg's reply in the same volume. Feinberg's paper is also discussed by Donald Van De Veer, 'Coercive Restraint of Offensive Actions', *Philosophy and Public Affairs,* 8 (1979).
51. Ibid., p. 102.
52. Devlin, p. 121.
53. Ibid., p. 120.
54. Cf. J. L. Mackie, *Ethics: Inventing Right and Wrong,* p. 182.

7. PATERNALISM

1. *On Liberty*, p. 137.
2. Ibid., p. 152.
3. Cf. Joel Feinberg, 'Legal Paternalism', *Canadian Journal of Philosophy*, 1 (1971).
4. *McCoy* (1953), cited by Graham Hughes, 'Consent in sexual offences', *Modern Law Review*, 25 (1962), pp. 683—4.
5. Glanville Williams, 'Consent and public policy', *The Criminal Law Review* (1962), p. 78.
6. For discussions of the connection between paternalism and the consent of the subject, see: Rosemary Carter, 'Justifying Paternalism', *Canadian Jouranl of Philosophy*, vii (1977); and John D. Hodson, 'The Principle of Paternalism', *American Philosophical Quarterly*, 14 (1977).
7. This problem is discussed by: John Rawls, *A Theory of Justice* (Oxford, 1972), pp. 249—50; Jeffrie G. Murphy, 'Incompetence and Paternalism', *Archives for Philosophy of Law and Social Philosophy*, lx (1974), pp. 482—3; and Rosemary Carter, op. cit., pp. 136—9.
8. *A Theory of Justice*, op. cit., ch. III.
9. Rawls applies his theory to the problem of paternalism in *A Theory of Justice*, pp. 248—50. See also: David A. J. Richards, *A Theory of Reasons for Action* (Oxford, 1971), pp. 192—5; and Jeffrie G. Murphy, op. cit.
10. On this point, see Laurence D. Houlgate, 'Children, Paternalism, and Rights to Liberty', in Onora O'Neill and William Ruddick (eds.), *Having Children* (Oxford, 1979).
11. *Collected Works of John Stuart Mill*, Vol. iii (Toronto and London, 1965), p. 947.
12. Ibid., p. 938.
13. *On Liberty*, p. 152.
14. These two examples are used to illustrate the same point by three different persons: Gerald Dworkin, 'Paternalism', in Richard A. Wasserstrom (ed.), *Morality and the Law* (Belmont, 1971), p. 125; Donald H. Regan, 'Justifications for Paternalism', in J. Ronald Pennock and John W. Chapman (eds.), *The Limits of Law*, Nomos XV (New York, 1974), p. 200; and Jonathan Glover, *Causing Death and Saving Lives* (Penguin, 1977), pp. 179—80.
15. For a discussion of the distinguishing features of slavery, see R. M. Hare. 'What Is Wrong with Slavery', *Philosophy and Public Affairs*, 8 (1979).
16. Donald H. Regan, 'Justifications for Paternalism', op. cit., Sect. iii.
17. Cf. 'Personal Identity', in John Perry (ed.), *Personal Identity* (Berkeley, Los Angeles, and London, 1975) and 'Later selves and moral principles', in Alan Montefiore (ed.), *Philosophy and Personal Relations* (London, 1973). See also Bernard Williams's comments in 'Persons, Character and Morality', in Amelie Oksenberg Rorty (ed.), *The Identities of Persons* (Berkeley, Los Angeles, and London, 1976).
18. 'Justifications for Paternalism', op. cit., p. 205.
19. Terry S. Kogan, 'The Limits of State Intervention: Personal Identity and Ultra-Risky Actions', *The Yale Law Journal*, 85 (1976).
20. Ibid., pp. 841—2.
21. Ibid., p. 837.

8. FREEDOM OF EXPRESSION

1. Stephen E. Norris seems to treat all of Mill's arguments as versions of the Avoidance of Mistake Argument. Cf. 'Being Free to Speak and Speaking

Freely', in Ted Honderich (ed.), *Social Ends and Political Means* (London, 1976).
2. John Locke, *A Letter Concerning Toleration* (New York, 1955), p. 19. The *Letter* was originally published in 1689.
3. John Morley, *Compromise* (London, 1891), pp. 247–8.
4. *Liberty, Equality, Fraternity* (Cambridge, 1967), p. 86.
5. 'Pledges', *The Examiner* (15 July 1832), p. 449.
6. J. W. N. Watkins, 'John Stuart Mill and the Liberty of the Individual', in D. Thomson (ed.), *Political Ideas* (London, 1966), pp. 173–4.
7. For an instructive discussion of the connection between the concept of harm and men's general wish to survive, see H. L. A. Hart, *The Concept of Law*, pp. 186–9. Cf. my discussion in Ch. 4.
8. Cf. Thomas I. Emerson, *The System of Freedom of Expression* (New York, 1970), pp. 328–36 *et passim*. This is a detailed and valuable discussion of 'the legal foundations for an effective system of freedom of expression' in the United States of America.
9. This raises 'the problem of the hostile audience'. For illuminating discussions, see Thomas I. Emerson, op. cit., pp. 336–42, and Geoffrey Marshall, *Constitutional Theory* (Oxford, 1971), pp. 160–7.
10. See: H. J. McCloskey, 'Liberty of Expression: its Grounds and Limits I', and D. H. Monro, 'Liberty of Expression: its Grounds and Limits II', *Inquiry*, 13 (1970); and Joel Feinberg, 'Limits to the Free Expression of Opinion', in Joel Feinberg and Hyman Gross (eds.), *Philosophy of Law* (Encino and Belmont, 1975).
11. Compare the exposition of Mill's ideas here with two recent important defences of freedom of expression by T. Scanlon, 'A Theory of Freedom of Expression', *Philosophy and Public Affairs*, 1 (1972), and by D. A. J. Richards, 'Free Speech and Obscenity Law: Towards a Moral Theory of the First Amendment', *University of Pennsylvania Law Review*, 123 (1974). A very different view is presented by Herbert Marcuse, 'Repressive Tolerance', in Robert Paul Wolff, Barrington Moore Jnr, Herbert Marcuse, *A Critique of Pure Tolerance* (London, 1969).
12. Anthony Quinton, 'Free Speech', *The Listener* (27 March 1969), p. 407.
13. *The Times* (13 July 1977).
14. Maurice Cranston, 'When we should censure the censors', *The Times Higher Education Supplement* (23 September 1977), p. 17.
15. Maurice Cranston, *What are Human Rights?* (London, 1973). p. 44.
16. *The Times* (13 July 1977).
17. Ibid.

9. MILL AND LIBERTY

1. Maurice Cowling, *Mill and Liberalism* (Cambridge, 1963), hereafter cited as *Mill and Liberalism*.
2. Shirley Letwin, *The Pursuit of Certainty* (Cambridge, 1965).
3. Ibid., p. 8.
4. John Stuart Mill, *Essays On Politics and Culture* (New York, 1963), ed. with introduction by Gertrude Himmelfarb, hereafter cited as *Politics and Culture*.
5. Gertrude Himmelfarb, *On Liberty and Liberalism: The Case of John Stuart Mill* (New York, 1974), hereafter cited as *On Liberty and Liberalism*.
6. Cowling's book has received much attention. J. C. Rees gives an account of the nature of these comments in 'The Reaction to Cowling on Mill', *The Mill News Letter*, Vol. i, No. 2 (1966). Rees has added his own well-argued and more detailed criticisms of Cowling in 'Was Mill For Liberty', *Political*

Studies, xiv (1966). An earlier paper by Rees is also relevant to the topic of this chapter: 'A Phase In The Development of Mill's Ideas on Liberty', *Political Studies,* vi (1958).

7. *Mill and Liberalism,* p. 104.
8. Ibid., p. 33.
9. *On Liberty,* p. 125.
10. *The Pursuit of Certainty,* p. 301.
11. Ibid., p. 308.
12. *On Liberty,* p. 148.
13. Ibid., p. 133.
14. *Mill and Liberalism,* p. 66.
15. *On Liberty,* p. 124.
16. *Mill and Liberalism,* pp. 25–6.
17. *The Later Letters of John Stuart Mill, 1849–1873, Collected Works,* Vol. xiv (Toronto and London, 1972), p. 294.
18. *Autobiography* (World's Classics Ed.), p. 216.
19. Ibid., pp. 140–1.
20. *Mill and Liberalism,* p. 117.
21. Ibid., p. 115.
22. *Politics and Culture,* p. 69.
23. Op. cit., p. 220.
24. *Politics and Culture,* p. xxiii.
25. The quotation is from Mill's essay, *Thoughts on Parliamentary Reform* which is included in *Politics and Culture,* p. 315.
26. *On Liberty and Liberalism,* p. 304 fn.
27. *Representative Government* (Everyman ed.), p. 193. A detailed and lucid discussion of this work is to be found in Dennis F. Thompson, *John Stuart Mill and Representative Government* (Princeton, 1976).
28. Ibid., p. 203.
29. Ibid., p. 207.
30. *Auguste Comte and Positivism* (Ann Arbor, 1961), p. 123.
31. Ibid., pp. 141–2.
32. Michael St. John Packe, *The Life of John Stuart Mill* (London, 1954), p. 68.
33. *Politics and Culture,* p. xv; *On Liberty and Liberalism,* p. 209.
34. *On Liberty and Liberalism,* p. 168.
35. Ibid., pp. 144 and 206 fn 42.
36. J. C. Rees, 'The Thesis of the Two Mills', *Political Studies,* xxv (1977), pp. 372, 375.
37. *On Liberty and Liberalism,* p. 181.
38. Ibid., p. 206 fn 42.
39. Ibid., p. 258.
40. Ibid., pp. 206–7
41. Ibid., p. 182.
42. *Collected Works,* Vol. xiv, p. 294.
43. *On Liberty and Liberalism,* p. 181.
44. Ibid., p. 152.
45. *Politics and Culture,* p. 239.
46. *On Liberty and Liberalism,* p. 82.
47. Ibid., pp. 83–4.
48. *Politics and Culture,* p. 263.
49. Ibid., p. 263.
50. Ibid., p. 263.
51. *On Liberty and Liberalism,* pp. 45–7, 76–80.

52. *Politics and Culture,* p. viii fn; *On Liberty and Liberalism,* p. 47 fn. The changes are collated in the *Collected Works,* Vol. x (Toronto and London, 1969), Appendix D, pp. 503—8.
53. But see Nicholas Capaldi, 'Censorship and Social Stability in J. S. Mill', *The Mill News Letter,* Vol. ix, No. 1 (1973).
54. A. Bain, *John Stuart Mill, a Criticism* (London, 1882), p. 57.
55. *Politics and Culture,* pp. 163—4.
56. Ibid., p. 168.
57. Ibid., p. 69.
58. Ibid., p. 73.
59. Ibid., p. 61.
60. *On Liberty and Liberalism,* pp. 44—5.
61. *Politics and Culture,* pp. xx; *On Liberty and Liberalism,* Ch. I.
62. This point is well made by Ronald Dworkin in *Taking Rights Seriously* (London, 1978), p. 261.
63. *On Liberty and Liberalism,* p. 299.
64. Ibid., p. 272.
65. Ibid., p. 168.
66. Ibid., p. 91.
67. Ibid., pp. 106—8.
68. Ibid., pp. 78—9.
69. *On Liberty,* p. 121.
70. *On Liberty and Liberalism,* pp. 91, 107, 139, 269.
71. *On Liberty,* p. 120.
72. Ibid., p. 132.
73. *The Life of John Stuart Mill,* p. 133.
74. *Politics and Culture,* p. 7.
75. *The Earlier Letters of John Stuart Mill, 1812—1848, Collected Works,* Vol. xii (Toronto and London, 1963), p. 77; hereafter cited as *Earlier Letters,* Vol. xii.
76. Ibid., p. 153. Cf. *Politics and Culture,* p. xii; and *On Liberty and Liberalism,* pp. 47—8.
77. *Earlier Letters,* Vol. xii, p. 46.
78. Ibid., p. 46.
79. *On Liberty,* p. 111.
80. *Earlier Letters,* Vol. xii, p. 124.
81. *On Liberty,* p. 94.
82. Ibid., p. 95.
83. *Politics and Culture,* p. 12.
84. Ibid., p. 36.
85. Ibid., p. 36.
86. *On Genius* in J. B. Schneewind (ed.), *Mill's Essays on Literature and Society* (New York and London, 1965), p. 101.
87. Ibid., p. 94.
88. *Examiner,* 1 July 1832, p. 417.
89. Bernard Wishy, *Prefaces to Liberty: Selected Writings of John Stuart Mill* (Boston, 1959).
90. Ibid., p. 99.
91. Ibid., p. 78.
92. Ibid., p. 71.
93. Ibid., pp. 146—7.
94. Ibid., p. 57.
95. *Politics and Culture,* p. 112.
96. Appendix to *Autobiography,* pp. 298—9.
97. Cf. *Earlier Letters,* Vol. xii, p. 40.

Bibliography

Works by Mill

The Collected Works of John Stuart Mill (Toronto and London, 1963–) contain the definitive editions of Mill's writings. The volumes published so far are:

- Vols. ii–iii : *Principles of Political Economy.* Introduction by V. W. Bladen; textual editor J. M. Robson.
- Vols. iv–v : *Essays on Economics and Society.* Introduction by Lord Robbins; textual editor J. M. Robson.
- Vols. vii–viii : *A System of Logic.* Introduction by R. F. McRae; textual editor J. M. Robson.
- Vol. ix : *An Examination of Sir William Hamilton's Philosophy.* Introduction by Alan Ryan; textual editor J. M. Robson.
- Vol. x : *Essays on Ethics, Religion, and Society.* Introduction by F. E. L. Priestley and D. P. Dryer; textual editor J. M. Robson.
- Vol. xi : *Essays on Philosophy and the Classics.* Introduction by F. E. Sparshott; textual editor J. M. Robson.
- Vols. xii–xiii : *Earlier Letters, 1812–1848.* Ed. Francis E. Mineka.
- Vols. xiv–xvii : *Later Letters, 1849–1873.* Ed. Francis E. Mineka.
- Vols. xviii–xix : *Essays on Politics and Society.* Introduction by Alexander Brady; textual editor J. M. Robson.

On Liberty appears in *Essays on Politics and Society, Collected Works,* Vol. xviii.

Utilitarianism appears in *Essays on Ethics, Religion and Society, Collected Works,* Vol. x.

References to *On Liberty* and *Utilitarianism* in the text are to the widely used Everyman edn., *Utilitarianism, Liberty, Representative Government.*

The following collections of Mill's essays are useful:

Himmelfarb, Gertrude (ed.), *Essays on Politics and Culture* (New York, 1963)

Rossi, Alice S (ed.), *Essays on Sex Equality by John Stuart Mill and Harriet Taylor Mill* (Chicago, 1970).

Schneewind, J. B. (ed.), *Mill's Ethical Writings* (New York and London, 1965).

Schneewind, J. B. (ed.), *Mill's Essays on Literature and Society* (New York and London, 1965).
Wishy, Bernard (ed.), *Prefaces to Liberty: Selected Writings of John Stuart Mill* (Boston, 1959).

The following works of Mill have also been cited in the text:

Autobiography (World's Classics Edn.). This contains an Appendix of some of Mill's Unpublished Speeches:
    'The Utility of Knowledge', 1823;
    'The British Constitution ', 1825;
    'Perfectibility', 1828;
    'Notes of Speech against Sterling', 1829;
    'The Church', 1829;
    'Secular Education', 1849.
August Comte and Positivism (Ann Arbor, 1961).
'Pledges', *The Examiner* (1 and 15 July 1832).

Works by Others

This lists all the items cited in the text plus a few additional items.

Anschutz, R. P., *The Philosophy of J. S. Mill* (London, 1963).
Bain, A., *John Stuart Mill, a Criticism* (London, 1882).
Baker, John, 'Utilitarianism and "Secondary Principles" ', *The Philosophical Quarterly*, 21 (1971).
Barry, Brian, *Political Argument* (London, 1965).
Benn, S. I. and Peters, R. S., *Social Principles and the Democratic State* (London, 1959).
Bentham, Jeremy, *An Introduction to the Principles of Morals and Legislation*, J. H. Burns and H. L. A. Hart (eds.), *The Collected Works of Jeremy Bentham* (London, 1970).
Berlin, Isaiah, *John Stuart Mill and the Ends of Life* (London, 1959); repr. in *Four Essays on Liberty* (Oxford, 1979).
Bogen, James and Daniel Farrell, 'Freedom and Happiness in Mill's Defence of Liberty', *The Philosophical Quarterly*, 28 (1978).
Britton, Karl, *John Stuart Mill* (Penguin, 1953).
Brock, Dan W., 'Recent Work in Utilitarianism', *American Philosophical Quarterly*, 10 (1973).
Brown, D. G., 'Mill on Liberty and Morality', *Philosophical Review*, lxxxi (1972).
—— 'What is Mill's Principle of Utility?', *Canadian Journal of Philosophy*, 3 (1973).
—— 'Mill on Harm to Others' Interests', *Political Studies*, xxvi (1978).

Capaldi, Nicholas, 'Censorship and Social Stability in J. S. Mill', *The Mill News Letter*, Vol. ix, No. 1 (1973).

Carter, Rosemary, 'Justifying Paternalism', *Canadian Journal of Philosophy*, viii (1977).

Conway, David A., 'Law, Liberty and Indecency', *Philosophy*, 49 (1974).

Cooper, W. E., Kai Nielsen, and Steven C. Patten (eds.), *New Essays on John Stuart Mill and Utilitarianism*, *Canadian Journal of Philosophy*, Suppl. Vol. v (Ontario, 1979). This interesting collection of essays appeared too late to be taken into account in the text.

Cowling, Maurice, *Mill and Liberalism* (Cambridge, 1963).

Cranston, Maurice, 'When we should censure the censors', *The Times Higher Education Supplement* (23 September 1977).

Cranston, Maurice, *What are Human Rights?* (London, 1973).

Devlin, Patrick, *The Enforcement of Morals* (London, 1965).

Downie, R. S., 'Mill on Pleasure and Self-Development', *The Philosophical Quarterly*, 16 (1966).

—— and Elizabeth Telfer, *Respect for Persons* (London, 1966).

Dworkin, Gerald, 'Paternalism', in Richard Wasserstrom (ed.), *Morality and the Law* (Belmont, 1971).

Dworkin, Ronald, *Taking Rights Seriously* (London, 1978).

Emerson, Thomas I., *The System of Freedom of Expression* (New York, 1970).

Feinberg, Joel, 'Legal Paternalism', *Canadian Journal of Philosophy*, 1 (1971).

—— ' "Harmless Immoralities" and Offensive Nuisances', in Norman S. Care and Thomas K. Trelogan (eds.), *Issues in Law and Morality* (Cleveland and London, 1973). See also Michael D. Bayles's comments and Feinberg's reply in same vol.

—— *Social Philosophy* (New Jersey, 1973).

—— 'Limits to the Free Expression of Opinion', in Joel Feinberg and Hyman Gross (eds.), *Philosophy of Law* (Encino and Belmont, 1975).

—— 'Harm to Self-Interest', in P. M. S. Hacker and J. Raz (eds.), *Law, Morality and Society: Essays in Honour of H. L. A. Hart*, (Oxford, 1977).

Friedman, Richard B., 'A New Exploration of Mill's Essay On Liberty', *Political Studies*, xiv (1966).

Friedrich, Carl J. (ed.), *Liberty* (New York, 1962).

Gewirth, Alan, *Reason and Morality* (Chicago and London, 1978).

Giddens, Anthony, (ed.), *Emile Durkheim: Selected Writings* (Cambridge, 1972).

Gildin, H., 'Mill's *On Liberty*', in J. Cropsey (ed.), *Ancients and Moderns: Essays on the Tradition of Political Philosophy in Honour of Leo Strauss* (New York, 1964).

Glover, Jonathan, *Causing Death and Saving Lives* (Penguin, 1977).
Halliday, R. J., 'Some Recent Interpretations of John Stuart Mill', *Philosophy*, 43 (1968); repr. in J. B. Schneewind (ed.), *Mill: A Collection of Critical Essays* (London, 1968).
—— *John Stuart Mill* (London, 1976).
Hare, R. M., 'Reply to "Liberals, Fanatics and Not-so-important-Bystanders" ', in B. Y. Khanbhai, R. S. Katz, and R. A. Pineau (eds.), Jowett Papers (1968—9).
—— 'Wrongness and Harm', in *Essays on the Moral Concepts* (london, 1972).
—— 'Ethical Theory and Utilitarianism', in H. D. Lewis (ed.), *Contemporary British Philosophy: Personal Statements*, 4th Series (London, 1976).
—— 'What Is Wrong with Slavery', *Philosophy and Public Affairs*, 8 (1979).
Harris, John, 'The Survival Lottery', *Philosophy*, 50 (1975).
Hart, H. L. A., 'Immorality and Treason', *The Listener* (30 July 1959); repr. in Richard A. Wasserstrom (ed.), *Morality and the Law* (Belmont, 1971).
—— *The Concept of Law* (Oxford, 1961).
—— *Law, Liberty and Morality* (London, 1963).
—— *The Morality of the Criminal Law* (Oxford, 1965).
—— 'Social Solidarity and the Enforcement of Morals', *University of Chicago Law Review*, 35 (1967).
—— 'Between Utility and Rights', in Alan Ryan (ed.), *The Idea of Freedom: Essays in Honour of Isaiah Berlin* (Oxford, 1979).
Hayek, F. A., *John Stuart Mill and Harriet Taylor: Their Friendship and Subsequent Marriage* (London, 1951).
Himmelfarb, Gertrude, Introduction to her edn. of Mill's *Essays On Politics and Culture* (New York, 1963).
—— *On Liberty and Liberalism: The Case of John Stuart Mill* (New York, 1974).
Hodson, John D., 'The Principle of Paternalism', *American Philosophical Quarterly*, 14 (1977).
Honderich, Ted, *Punishment, the Supposed Justifications* (London, 1969).
—— 'The Worth of J. S. Mill *On Liberty*', *Political Studies*, xxii (1974).
Houlgate, L. D., 'Children, Paternalism and Rights to Liberty', in Onora O'Neill and William Ruddick (eds.), *Having Children* (Oxford 1979).
Hughes, Graham, 'Consent in sexual offences', *Modern Law Review*, 25 (1962).
Kendall, Willmore, 'The "Open Society" and Its Fallacies', in Peter Radcliff (ed.), *Limits of Liberty: Studies of Mill's On Liberty* (Belmont, 1966).

Kleinig, John, 'Crime and the Concept of Harm', *American Philosophical Quarterly*, 15 (1978).

Kogan, Terry S., 'The Limits of State Intervention: Personal Identity and Ultra-Risky Actions', *The Yale Law Journal*, 85 (1976).

Ladenson, Robert F., 'Mill's Conception of Individuality', *Social Theory and Practice*, 4 (1977).

Letwin, Shirley, *The Pursuit of Certainty* (Cambridge, 1965).

Locke, John, *A Letter Concerning Toleration* (New York, 1955).

Long, Douglas, *Bentham on Liberty* (Toronto, 1977).

Lucas, J. R., *The Principles of Politics* (Oxford, 1966).

Lukes, Steven, 'Durkheim's "Individualism and the Intellectuals"', *Political Studies*, xvii (1969).

—— *Emile Durkheim, His Life and Work* (London, 1973).

—— *Individualism* (Oxford, 1973).

Lyons, David, 'Mill's Theory of Morality', *Nous*, 10 (1976).

—— 'Human Rights and the General Welfare', *Philosophy and Public Affairs*, 6 (1977).

—— 'Mill's Theory of Justice', in Alvin I. Goldman and Jaegwon Kim (eds.), *Values and Morals* (Dordrecht, 1978).

Mackie, J. L., *Ethics: Inventing Right and Wrong* (Penguin, 1977).

—— 'Can there be a Right-Based Moral Theory?', *Midwest Studies in Philosophy*, iii (1978).

Marcuse, Herbert, 'Repressive Tolerance', in Robert Paul Wolff, Barrington Moore Jr., Herbert Marcuse, *A Critique of Pure Tolerance* (London, 1969).

Marshall, Geoffrey, *Constitutional Theory* (Oxford, 1971).

McCloskey, H. J., 'Mill's Liberalism', *The Philosophical Quarterly*, 13 (1963).

—— 'Mill's Liberalism – A Rejoinder to Mr. Ryan', *The Philosophical Quarterly*, 16 (1966).

—— *John Stuart Mill: A Critical Study* (London, 1971).

—— 'Liberty of Expression: its Grounds and Limits I', *Inquiry*, 13 (1970)

Mitchell, Basil, *Law Morality and Religion in a Secular Society* (London, 1967).

—— 'Law and the Protection of Institutions', in *The Proper Study*, Royal Institute of Philosophy Lectures, Vol. 4 (1969–70).

Monro, D. H., 'Liberty of Expression: its Grounds and Limits II', *Inquiry*, 13 (1970).

—— 'Mill's Third Howler', in Robert Brown and C. D. Rollins (eds.), *Contemporary Philosophy in Australia* (London, 1969).

Morley, John, 'Mr. Mill's Doctrine of Liberty', *Fortnightly Review*, (1 August 1873).

—— *Compromise* (London, 1891).

Murphy, J. G., 'Incompetence and Paternalism', *Archives for Philosophy of Law and Social Philosophy*, lx (1974).

Nagel, Ernest, 'The Enforcement of Morals', in Paul Kurtz (ed.), *Moral Problems in Contemporary Society* (Englewood Cliffs, 1969).

Norris, Stephen E., 'Being Free to Speak and Speaking Freely', in Ted Honderich (ed.), *Social Ends and Political Means* (London, 1976).

Packe, M. St. John, *The Life of John Stuart Mill* (London, 1954).

Pappe, H. O., *John Stuart Mill and the Harriet Taylor Myth* (Melbourne, 1960).

Parfit, Derek, 'Personal Identity', in John Perry (ed.), *Personal Identity* (Berkeley, Los Angeles, and London, 1975).

—— 'Later selves and moral principles', in Alan Montefiore (ed.), *Philosophy and Personal Relations* (London, 1973).

Partridge, P. H., *Consent and Consensus* (London, 1971).

Quinton, Anthony, 'Free Speech', *The Listener* (27 March 1969).

Rawls, John, *A Theory of Justice* (Oxford, 1972).

Raz, Joseph, 'Professor Dworkin's Theory of Rights', *Political Studies*, 26 (1978).

Rees, J. C., *Mill and His Early Critics* (Leicester, 1956).

—— 'A Phase In The Development of Mill's Ideas On Liberty', *Political Studies*, vi (1958).

—— 'A Re-Reading of Mill On Liberty', *Political Studies*, viii (1960); repr. with a new postscript, in Peter Radcliff (ed.), *Limits of Liberty: Studies of Mill's On Liberty* (Belmont, 1966).

—— 'Individualism and Individual Liberty', *Il Politico*, 26 (1961).

—— 'The Reaction to Cowling on Mill', *The Mill News Letter*, Vol. i, No. 2 (1966).

—— 'Was Mill for Liberty?', *Political Studies*, xiv (1966).

—— 'The Thesis of the Two Mills', *Political Studies*, xxv (1977).

Regan, Donald H., 'Justifications for Paternalism', in J. Ronald Pennock and John W. Chapman (eds.), *The Limits of Law* (New York, 1974).

Reynolds, Noel B., 'The Enforcement of Morals and the Rule of Law', *Georgia Law Review*, ii (1977).

Richards, David A. J., *A Theory of Reasons for Action* (Oxford, 1971).

—— 'Free Speech and Obscenity Law: Towards a Moral Theory of the First Amendment', *University of Pennsylvania Law Review*, 123 (1974).

Robson, John M., *The Improvement of Mankind: The Social and Political Thought of John Stuart Mill* (Toronto, 1968).

Ryan, Alan, 'Mr. McCloskey on Mill's Liberalism', *The Philosophical Quarterly*, 14 (1964).

—— 'John Stuart Mill's Art of Living', *The Listener* (21 October 1965).

—— *The Philosophy of John Stuart Mill* (London, 1970).

—— *John Stuart Mill* (London, 1974).

Sartorius, Rolf E., *Individual Conduct and Social Norms* (Belmont, 1975).

Scanlon, T., 'A Theory of Freedom of Expression', *Philosophy and Public Affairs*, i (1972).

Singer, Peter, 'Utility and the Survival Lottery', *Philosophy*, 50 (1977).

Smart, J. J. C., 'Extreme and Restricted Utilitarianism', in Samuel Gorovitz (ed.), *Mill: Utilitarianism, with Critical Essays* (Indianapolis, 1971).

—— 'Hedonistic and Ideal Utilitarianism', *Midwest Studies in Philosophy*, iii (1978).

—— and Bernard Williams, *Utilitarianism: For and Against* (Cambridge, 1973).

Stephen, James Fitzjames, *Liberty, Equality, Fraternity*, ed. with introduction and notes by R. J. White (Cambridge, 1967).

—— *A History of the Criminal Law of of England*, Vol. ii (London, 1883).

Stephen, Leslie, *The Life of Sir James Fitzjames Stephen* (London, 1895).

—— *The English Utilitarians*, Vol. iii, *John Stuart Mill* (London, 1900).

Strawson, P. F., 'Social Morality and Individual Ideal', *Philosophy*, 36 (1961).

Taylor, Richard, *Freedom, Anarchy, and the Law* (New Jersey, 1973).

The Times (13 July 1977).

Thompson, Dennis F., *John Stuart Mill and Representative Government* (Princeton, 1976).

Van De Veer, Donald, 'Coercive Restraint of Offensive Actions', *Philosophy and Public Affairs*, 8 (1979).

Watkins, J. W. N., 'John Stuart Mill and the Liberty of the Individual', in D. Thomson (ed.), *Political Ideas* (London, 1966)

Williams, Bernard, 'Persons, Character and Morality', in Amelie Oksenberg Rorty (ed.), *The Identities of Persons* Berekeley, Los Angeles, and London, 1976).

Williams, G. L.; 'Mill's Principle of Liberty', *Political Studies*, xxiv (1976).

Williams, Glanville, 'Consent and public policy', *The Criminal Law Review* (1962).

Wolff, Robert Paul, *The Poverty of Liberalism* (Boston, 1969).

Wollheim, Richard, 'John Stuart Mill and the Limits of State Action', *Social Research*, 40 (1973).

—— 'Introduction', *John Stuart Mill: Three Essays on Liberty, Representative Government, The Subjection of Women* (London, 1975).

—— 'John Stuart Mill and Isaiah Berlin: The Ends of Life and the Preliminaries of Morality', in Alan Ryan (ed.), *The Idea of Freedom: Essays in Honour of Isaiah Berlin* (Oxford, 1979).

Index of Proper Names

193